Bobbi —
The last shall
be 1st

Linda Chavez

Unleashed To Learn

Empowering Students To Learn at Full Capacity

Linda C. Aronson

Copyright © 2013 by Linda C. Aronson
Cover Photo by Linda C. Aronson

ISBN 978-0-7414-8196-2 Paperback
ISBN 978-0-7414-8197-9 eBook
Library of Congress Control Number: 2012922757

Printed in the United States of America

Published February 2013

INFINITY PUBLISHING
1094 New DeHaven Street, Suite 100
West Conshohocken, PA 19428-2713
Toll-free (877) BUY BOOK
Local Phone (610) 941-9999
Fax (610) 941-9959
Info@buybooksontheweb.com
www.buybooksontheweb.com

Praise for Unleashed to Learn!

Every student in America should have the experience of a capstone project. In *Unleashed to Learn* Linda Aronson provides educators with a sound rationale for why this is true, a clear and accessible set of steps for how to structure them, and many compelling examples of what they look like when done well. This is a book for practitioners, policy makers, and parents who want to see students engage in work with the power to shape their lives for the better.

—**Scott Hartl**, President & CEO of Expeditionary Learning, New York, N.Y.

If you are still seeking a strong argument in support of student-centered learning, look no further. *Unleashed to Learn* is a powerfully written book that combines thoughtful insight about how best to design and support learning along with some of the most compelling stories of student success I've ever read. This is an inspiring must-read.

—**Mark Kostin**, Ed.D. Associate Director, Great Schools Partnership, Portland, Maine.

Unleashed to Learn represents a transformational change in a particularly insightful district, staff, and emerging generation of graduates. Aronson referenced the quote, "Education is to draw forth, not impose upon" which accurately captures the Senior Seminar/Capstone experience she developed. As an observer/evaluator of this secondary education cultural change, I witnessed Aronson nurture the concept into a manifestation of self-efficacy within each of her learners. She unleashed her students to learn and provided personalized opportunities to address the impossible.

 Unleashed to Learn provides a rational and emotional blueprint for others to analyze, adopt, and develop into a lifelong memorable experience for each learner.

—**Don Siviski**, Maine State Superintendent of Instruction.

Unleashed to Learn simultaneously took me backward and forward—backward to relive the mental and emotional transformation I underwent as a Capstone student and unleashed learner and forward with hope for the future of education in America.

When I compared experiences with my peers in higher education who had never truly experienced the empowerment of self-directed learning, I knew Mrs. Aronson was on to something. Now, after reading *Unleashed to Learn*, I am sure she is.

Unleashed to Learn brings raw learning to life with stories of students exploring their passions on their own terms. This book is not just for academics—it is for everyone with a drive to stretch their imagination, break out of their comfort zones, and inspire learning in others.

—**Alexa Lightner**, former Capstone student, M.S. in Professional Communications, strategic communicator for start-ups and social enterprise.

I could not put this book down! Aronson captures the dramatic and tangible impact Capstone has on students' learning and their lives. Knowing the students and their experiences, I see now that a high school diploma is an institutional acknowledgment of achievement. "Capping" is a personal acknowledgment of even greater achievements. Entrusting students to take charge of their own learning transformed how we "do school."

—**Stephen MacDougall**, M.S.Ed, CAS, retired principal.

As a former student of Linda Aronson, the empowerment that I developed in her classroom has been reinvigorated by *Unleashed to Learn*. Once I cracked open the book I didn't put it down until I finished the whole thing. Fearless writing. Daring. Revolutionary yet simple to embrace, *Unleashed to Learn* is credible and real. "This is a tested method and here's the proof that it works!" The featured Capstones kept me excited throughout the book. *Unleashed to Learn* is relevant to not only students; it will ignite anyone who is brazen enough to raise the bar, and reclaim their own future. If these kids can be motivated to change their lives and community, you can too.

—**Daniel Voner**, Juris Doctor Candidate at West Virginia University School of Law.

Unleashed to Learn is a wonderful testament to what happens when you put students in the driver's seat of their learning and a good reminder of some of the most important things students can learn in life—taking ownership of their learning and fulfilling goals.

Aronson's book is an inspiration for educators who want to create an engaging environment that focuses on the process of learning. When you engage a student, you can engage a school, and you can engage a community. Powerful celebrations of learning will undoubtedly follow. Linda Aronson's journey to facilitate learning opportunities is proof of contagious engagement.

—**Jennifer Payne**, M.S. Director of Internship Program and Career Resource Center and Faculty, Sterling College, Craftsbury Common, Vermont.

Dedication

To Judith B. Crispell

*My mother,
and my inspiration for education.*

Contents

To The Reader

Welcome to the future of education. It has already arrived! This book is about the need to see and support fully the innate desire and drive within students to learn and create at full capacity. Children are hardwired to learn—it is their birthright. Their appetite to learn is insatiable in the first years of life. But as students progress through school, they sacrifice their innate curiosity, imagination, and creativity for external approval and rewards in a sorting and ranking system. Such sacrifices make school a perpetuation of the past and a breeding ground of mediocrity for many.

Years ago I dreamed of a school where students, upon entering, are asked one question: "What do *you want* to learn?" The students know that this is a key question. They know their answer must come from deep inside them, from their core. It must be something that they can give their whole self to—body, mind, and heart. An acceptable answer must be a match for their interests, proclivities, intelligences, and curiosity. Once the match is made, a plan is set in motion and the necessary resources in terms of people, facilities, and materials are gathered from within the school and wider community to enable the student to learn what he most wants to learn. When new learning is evident, the student presents to the school and wider community what she has learned for the benefit of all. The student is then honored in a coveted community celebration.

This is not futuristic. My dream came true. My book, *Unleashed to Learn*, is how it happened through the Capstone, not as an end in itself but as a catalyst and contagion for cultural change. Without turning an entire school upside down or inside out, it provides the illustrative evidence for the transformational effect of an approach to learning that is student-centered, relevant, real world, and applied.

I used to tell my students, "You are the future in education—you are the forerunners." To make this come true, I promised to write this book to make it real in the now, rather than a dream for the future. My students *were* the future.

Whenever I tell people about the Capstone, they always light up. "Hey, that sounds fantastic!" "Where do you do that?" "All learning should happen that way." "Where can I get information about the Capstone program?" This made it even clearer why I needed to write this book.

Parents who know education must change and anguish over the mismatch between school and their child(ren), have pleaded with me to "Hurry and get your book out, it is needed—Now!"

A mentor for one of my students asked, "How come I didn't get cool assignments like that in high school?"

Even my principal once told me, "You know, you have the best job in the building."

* * *

The audience for *Unleashed to Learn* is aspiring teachers, current teachers, administrators, high school students, parents, and college faculty.

The book is organized so it can be read in "teacher time" or in short snatches. If you read nonfiction anything like I do, I leaf through the book reading what strikes me at the moment rather than progressing from front to back.

The *Introduction* synthesizes the breathtaking breakthroughs of new understandings about human intelligence and capacity that are prompting the field of education to align its theories and practices to this expanded view of the human mind. These new understandings also provide support for the concepts of whole intelligence for learning and creating at full capacity in *Unleashed to Learn.*

Shift in Six (Part II) tells the story of how six consecutive senior classes in a small but recognized public high school in central Maine raised the Capstone initiative to become a showcase model for student-centered, self-directed, differentiated, interdisciplinary, and experiential learning. I call it *full-circle learning* for short.

Full-Circle Learning at Full Capacity (Part III) details all the components of the Capstone model for full-circle learning. This is the "how to" section of the book, that comes alive with illustrated examples from real students, teachers, and mentors. It concludes with a short chapter on the administration of the Capstone highlighting why it is a standout in education for students of the twenty-first century.

Power at the Core (Part IV), a brief chapter, focuses on the source of personal power, will, and action needed to undertake a Capstone. The Capstone is a means to develop this essential personal power and will and then channel it for positive purposes and transformational outcomes.

Creating a Capstone (Part V), combined with the earlier Senior Capstone vignettes, form the heart of the book. The specific Capstones were selected for their wide diversity of topics and varied learning processes. The selected Capstones also represent the full spectrum of student achievement levels ranging from those who struggle to graduate all the way to the valedictorian as evidence that full-circle learning is doable for all students. Selection was also based on the transformative and empowering value of the Capstone, either for the student or the program. Some of the most phenomenal transformations were too personal to include in the book. All student work that is quoted or referenced in the book is archived with the author. Each former student, now alumnus or alumna, gave permission to illustrate his or her Capstone in the book. In terms of names, Dan Voner was the only alumnus who specifically requested that I use his real and full name (see "Maple Street").

Unleashed to Teach (Part IV) are a few snapshots, taken inside a twenty-first-century classroom, that challenge long-held conventions of school culture in order to foster a more open environment for learning and creating as part of the transformation already underway in education today.

Last Words is the culmination of an initiative that had come full circle and of a dream come true.

In the *Afterword, Self-Designed Learning: A Growing Option in Higher Education,* I discuss how the individualized and interdisciplinary course of study option in higher education is in essence the same model for learning as the Senior Capstone. This option has caught fire and is restructuring the long-standing boundaries between traditional disciplines in academics at the college level.

Unleashed to Learn is the inspiring story and illustration of what students find both in themselves and in the world when they learn and create at full capacity. As students reclaim their birthright, the innate desire and drive to learn, we bear witness to the transformation of our students and education itself. I invite you to experience for yourself the phenomenon of what is possible when students are unleashed to learn.

Part 1

Introduction and Background

The meaning of education is a leading out, a drawing-forth;
not an imposition on somebody, *but eliciting of what is within him.*
Sir Arthur Thomas Quiller-Couch (1863-1944)

1

Learning at Full Capacity

Einstein said it first, so I can dare to say it too: everyone is a genius. Meaning, everyone has something to offer the world that no one else can offer in quite the same way. I apply the definition of *genius* as defined by "a single strongly marked capacity" that I will refer to as "full capacity" for short.[1] This full capacity is not surface stuff—it lies deep within, at the core, and must be drawn out to find expression. I trust that students can reach their genius within or their full capacity and bring it forward if they are trusted, supported, and asked to do so. That, I believe, is the highest calling of education and what the whole fuss in education is all about. It's the place we want to go with students but are not sure how to get there.

We are all talking around it and struggling to find it. We put our trust in multiple-choice standardized testing to show evidence of learning, regardless of whether what is tested is meaningful, useful, or a match for the students' proclivities or relevant to their lives or goals. If the scores are high, we in education have done our job; we have succeeded. If the scores are low, the goal is to improve the scores. We trust tests over students and even worse, over ourselves. We have relinquished our roles as professional and creative educators to the big business interests of standardized testing.

In education we talk incessantly about student engagement. We intuitively know that when students are fully engaged, learning is happening. This gives us hope and keeps us breathing. We want to resuscitate ourselves and our students back to life where there is an active love for learning—our forgotten birthright. We yearn for learning to flow, to be dynamic, an equal exchange of energy and fresh ideas between student and teacher—we want to be curious and excited about learning again. We know the futility of force. It's exhausting and it just backfires.

The pressure is on, as it should be. It is time to let go of control and unleash students to learn at their full capacity to find their genius within. I repeat, that is the higher calling of education. If we set our course on that, even if we as teachers and students falter, take wrong turns or get lost from time to time, at least we are heading in the right direction. We will probably have to throw some baggage (in terms of curriculum, instructional methods, and roles) overboard if it is deemed no longer relevant—just vestiges of the past—in order to lighten the load and make way for the new.

In all honesty, as a self-styled teacher I was often confused about my role as the facilitator of the Senior Capstone, a self-designed, interdisciplinary, and experiential approach to learning. The Senior Capstone, the centerpiece of this book, was by its very nature skewed towards process. Over and over again, I had to trust, hold my breath, and believe that my students would come through, because I was not wholly in charge—I was facilitating but not controlling the process. If I tried to control it, my efforts always backfired. It was a continuous process of letting go, trusting, supporting, guiding, and encouraging students to pursue what most interested them. This requires continuously widening the circle of learning.

Not until I came across the adage, *Education is to draw forth, not impose upon*, did it finally all click. That one phrase encapsulated and legitimized what I was actually doing but had no name for in the sea of a curriculum driven by content. To empower students to learn at full capacity necessitates that we, as educators, guide them through the full circle of learning and creating. I repeat once again: to help students find what makes them come alive and what they can give their whole self to, is the highest calling of education.

Expansion of Human Intelligence

We are moving into an age when our beliefs about intelligence are not only expanding but also mutating. We are in the process of reintegrating what we had separated and pulled apart through the ever-expanding knowledge of human capacity. We are "rediscovering" that the whole human system is teeming with intelligence and that the brain does not contain the whole of human intelligence. All intelligences and their loci are intricately and intimately related—are dynamic, with infinite possibilities. We are learning through social and biological sciences and technology the full extent and spectrum of human capacity to learn and create.

I think many would agree that the field of education is undergoing a metamorphosis. Psychology—neuroscience in particular—and education are merging into a new science of learning. This is transforming the field of education so that it can align itself with the breathtaking revelations about human capacity.

In just the last two or three decades, our understanding of the scope and the very nature of human intelligence has expanded and been redefined. To review, it was the Harvard developmental psychologist and best-selling author Howard Gardner who introduced the concept of multiple intelligences to the field of education back in the 1980s. Gardner's nine different intelligences challenged the field of education to reassess its primary focus on logical and linguistic intelligences to include the underplayed bodily/kinesthetic, visual/spatial, existential, naturalist, interpersonal, and intrapersonal intelligences.[2] Coupled with the advent and expansion of multiple intelligences was the acknowledgment of different learning styles, overlapping with multiple intelligences and reinforcing the idea that learning happens through various systems in the body and different ways of interacting with the environment. Again, the field of education was challenged to expand beyond a predominant reliance on the auditory and visual senses for learning to include the equally legitimate and multiply used physical, social, and solitary learning styles.

In the 1990s, psychologist and best-selling author Daniel Goleman further expanded the domain of intelligence in his description and exploration of social and emotional intelligences. By highlighting these intelligences as particularly relevant to happiness and success in life, Goleman not only expanded the field of psychology, but also challenged the prevailing belief that the intellect—the application of logic— was the superior intelligence.[3]

To accommodate the expansion of multiple intelligences and learning styles, new models for learning and teaching have emerged—models such as the differentiated, interdisciplinary, wholistic, and experiential approaches to education illustrated in this book through the Capstone. The use and blending of these models open the way for more natural and authentic learning. They supersede the strict and artificial boundaries between subjects and disciplines. After all, life itself is interdisciplinary. These new models have shifted the spotlight in education from a strict focus on content to a broader view that includes context, and from an exclusive concern with product to include process or how learning happens. The process of learning is learning in itself.

The expansion of intelligences, learning styles, and new models for teaching and learning are all moving from an educational system that was limited, exclusionary, and in many ways unnatural, towards a vision of education that finally embraces, inspires, and develops a fuller human capacity with a myriad of expressions.

In recent years, pressure has mounted for education to teach students to be life-long learners as is necessary for living in the rapidly changing world of the twenty-first century. The focus of education has become learning to learn—preparing students for the unknown world of the future. There is a particular emphasis on innovation and creativity applicable to all areas deemed necessary for competing in the global economy and the developing idea age, successor to the information age.

The incorporation of multiple intelligences, intersensory learning styles, and the emphasis on learning to learn was the perfect segue for brain-based learning promoted by Eric Jensen, Renate and Geoffrey Caine, David Sousa and others.[4]

Brain-based learning is the offspring of the revelations in brain development and functioning through the emergence of imaging technology. Just as Gardner and Goleman challenged the reality of a finite IQ or intellect, neuroscience continues to reveal the scientific evidence for the dynamic nature or plasticity of brain development and function throughout life.

This neuroplasticity addresses the dynamic and infinite versus static or finite capacity of the brain to grow, develop, change, and reorganize itself through stimulation, use, and meaningful experience. Neuroplasticity is not a new concept; it dates back to the 1960s as the theoretical foundation for restorative therapies in health care. Today, with the ascent of neuroscience, neuroplasticity has become scientifically substantiated and been adopted and popularized in education through brain-based learning.

Central to the principles of brain-based learning is the "rediscovery" that cognition does not function autonomously but is in fact strongly affected and strengthened by daily exercise and movement as well as positive emotional states. Optimal levels of multisensory stimulation and challenge light up the brain, as do novelty and the arousal of curiosity. Self-initiation, doing, meaningful activity and experience light up even more of the brain. Repetition and rehearsal reinforce learning and memory. Executive functioning within the prefrontal cortex of the brain, which develops during adolescence and young adulthood, has understandably received much attention since this high cortical center, so relevant to learning, modulates self-regulation of behavior, critical and creative thinking, decision making, planning, and executing complex tasks.

Given all the above, it is only the *application* of knowledge that generates meaningful experience and true learning. For learning experiences to be meaningful they must incorporate the whole human system: mind, body, and heart. In *The Heart of Higher Education,* authors Parker Palmer and Arthur Zajonc remind us that "If we would expand the worldview that supports education, we can find no better place to begin than by opening ourselves to the full scope of human experience. Life comprises an infinitely rich array of sensorial, emotional, and intellectual experiences."[5]

Whereas brain-based learning—in fact, the entire field of education itself—has the mind as its domain, there are other loci in the human body where vital and significant information is received, perceived, and then processed within the whole system—those being the heart and the gastrointestinal systems. I would contend that it the combination of all three systems: head, heart, and gut, that is the whole of human intelligence or whole intelligence and is the trilogy of full human capacity.

As the reductionist thinkers we are in the Western world, we like to pull apart the pieces that make up a human being— seeing the interdependent systems as separate but unequal, with the mind and its associated organ, the brain, reigning. But the unquestioned supremacy and dominance of the brain as the seat of highest intelligence has been challenged by the ongoing scientific study of heart intelligence. In recent years a fuller understanding of heart intelligence has emerged and has been put into practice in areas of health, well-being, performance, and yes, education—most notably by the Heartmath Solution Institute, founded by Doc Lew Childre, author of *The Heartmath Solution.*[6] In fact, the heart is known to have the largest energy field in the human body, greater than either the brain or the gut. It is the heart that the human system most naturally entrains for its greatest coherence or harmonious state.[7] The heart imagines and envisions; the head thinks and plans; the gut intuits and acts. When the head, heart, and gut are communicating and cooperating, they are a dynamic team.[8] It takes all three—head, heart, and gut to learn at full capacity.

There is an old adage that we use when someone goes above and beyond, works at full capacity for the love and joy of it. We say, "He really put his heart into it." Those words were the seal of approval the principal gave to a Capstone in which the student was learning and creating at his full capacity and by doing so, excelled.

Thanks to the relatively new science of epigenetics, we now know that not only are we not limited by our brains, but neither are we limited by our inherited genes or DNA, long believed to be finite or set for life, just as IQ was once thought to be. The pioneering field of epigenetics is exploring the scientific evidence for how our thoughts, beliefs, intentions, and attitudes alter gene expression, affecting among other things our capacity to learn. School director Greg Whitby, in the YouTube video entitled "Twenty-First Century Pedagogy," speaks to this ability to change the expression of our genes by calling for new DNA for teachers. He explains that the old pedagogy of the past century is deeply ingrained because it has lasted over a century. He describes the new pedagogical paradigm for the twenty-first century—that is, a new pedagogical DNA—in which both students and teachers are active co-constructors of learning and knowledge.[9]

This has been a quick overview of emerging and converging forces that challenge the field of education to create models for learning that can fully support the ever-expanding knowledge of human capacity. *Unleashed to Learn* is the story and illustration of how students across the scholastic-achievement spectrum took hold of the Capstone challenge and demonstrated a capacity to learn and create at a fuller capacity or beyond what others or they themselves believed possible.

The Capstone is a full-circle model for learning and creating that embraces the trilogy of human capacity—the head, the heart, and the gut. In the language of education, it is the melding of student-centered and driven, differentiated, multidisciplinary, experiential and applied learning approaches. Learning at full capacity happens when students are unleashed to learn, unlimited by content or context and free of any barriers to their natural curiosity, their intelligences, and their drive to learn and create.

All students are capable of their own brand of genius. It is just a matter of finding and then activating it. In the words of Galileo Galilei, "You cannot teach a man anything; you can only help him find it within himself."

2

Innate Intelligence & Learning to Create

If the aforementioned multiple intelligences already discussed are not enough, I add one more—innate intelligence. There is an innate intelligence that is generated not by thought but by energy. Innate intelligence is swifter than thought, so it will not be intercepted. Innate intelligence acts as a guiding system to something vitally important, highly significant, or rich with truth. When triggered, innate intelligence ignites an energy surge that puts one on full alert. One cannot help but *pay attention*!

Unleashed to Learn is an outcome of this innate intelligence. While I was browsing in a local bookstore years ago, energy shot through me as I leafed through a book entitled *The Path of Least Resistance*. It contained author Robert Fritz's principles for and process of creating. At the first opportunity, I was in Fritz's worldwide training course on creating that he applies to all types of business, to health, to the arts, to relationships, and yes, to education.

Fritz asserts that creating is the highest level of human function and that the process of creating can be taught. This process for creating became, in part, the foundation for the full-circle learning model of the Senior Capstone, a model that facilitates the practice of innovation and creativity considered vital for success in the twenty-first century.

Key to learning to create is moving through the *entire* cycle of creating. That is what makes it transformational. Simply put, the cycle begins with choice, moves through the process and phases of new learning and growth that is then integrated towards a point of completion. The process is cyclic rather than linear because completion sets off another cycle of creating.

Fritz acknowledges that traditional education is more about teaching youth to respond, fit in, and adapt to society the way it is than about teaching students to create the life they want and change society for the better.[1]

The desire and ability to create do not need to be reserved for the arts or for a special few. Creating applies to all people and in all areas of interest, aspiration, and endeavor. According to Fritz, the secret of creating is not a process of selection from existing options external to oneself. Rather, the secret to creating is to Make It Up! "Creative people make up what they create."[2] Fritz notes that "making up" new ideas is usually not encouraged in the school setting. The set curriculum is what matters.

As a facilitator of the Senior Capstone, I was able to gauge where students were within the creative cycle as well as where the program itself was in its own development. Whereas a student went through the full creative cycle in six months to complete a Capstone, it took six years for the program to pass through the entire creative cycle from an initiative to its full development. I used Fritz's language and concepts of creating with my students, concepts such as building momentum, resolving creative tension, and progressing through the creative cycle. This helped legitimize creating as consisting of equal parts knowledge, process, and skill.

Innate intelligence was set off again when I first heard the perspectives and assertions of Ken Robinson, author of *Out of Our Minds* and *The Element: How Finding Your Passion*

Changes Everything. Robinson is shaking the world of education with his humorous and witty straight talk about traditional education. His assertion that schools kill students' creativity through right and wrong answers, testing, and one-size-fits-all education has really hit a nerve.[3] At the time of this writing there were over a million views of his "Schools Kill Creativity" TED lecture.[4] Robinson believes, as Fritz knows and teaches, that creating, can be taught and is not limited to any special group.[5]

Robinson is clear that creating is synonymous with *doing*. "You could not be creative unless you were actually *doing* something."[6] Robinson concurs with Fritz that creativity is applied to all areas of endeavor such as business, science, technology, and education, not only the arts. The area does not matter as long as there is value in what one is creating.

My innate intelligence surged once again when the twenty-first-century edition of *Bloom's Taxonomy*, a widely used guide for educators regarding levels of thinking, was shared by our school coach, who was urging all faculty across disciplines to engage students more fully through higher levels of thinking—specifically, analysis and synthesis. Interestingly, right in time for the new millennium, *creating* was not only added to *Bloom's Taxonomy* but also placed at the very top as the *highest* level of thinking. Fritz would be proud. Creating was no longer a peripheral, nonessential sideliner in education, but its very apex.

Creating is getting serious attention in education today. In our democratic society, legislation means legitimization. In 2010, public schools in Massachusetts were required by law to teach creativity and teachers are rated "on their ability to teach, encourage, and foster creativity in students."[7] Support for the legislation was built on the premise that we now live in a creative economy and that employers identify "creativity as a requisite skill."[8] Creativity is now understood to be an essential twenty-first-century skill that can and should be taught in schools, and that this requires both the opportunity and the practice. It will be interesting now to see how far this new emphasis on creativity will go within the educational system and whether other states will follow Massachusetts's lead.

In higher education, Hampshire College opened a new Creativity Center in 2011 with a gift from Eileen Fisher, the parent of a new graduate, who built a multimillion-dollar fashion line after starting out with just $350.[9] Hampshire College's motto, "To know is not enough," reflects both strong support for creativity and also an understanding that creativity is vital for becoming a visionary, an innovator, or an agent of social change.[10]

The Capstone is a model for learning to create and creating to learn in any area of interest through moving through the entire cycle of creating—full circle and at full capacity.

3

The School Scene

School is too often seen as something to get through, something you just have to do. Everyone does. It is all preparatory for the future. You need to do such and such so you can get into college or get a job. Required curriculum—one size fits all. It is too often a passive process of "sit and get."

In school, daily life is divided into "subjects." At 9:00 am you are in English and at 10:00 you are in algebra. Eleven o'clock is bio, and after lunch, history. Regimented and always the same routine; it's no wonder that, far too often, students equate school with boredom or stress. And they see far too much of their school work as irrelevant, not at all like the "real world," as students like to say.

And who's to blame? Who is responsible? We all are. We have unwittingly accepted all this as the status quo and even thought it necessary to becoming "educated."

Learn About versus Learning

The challenge of the educational system today is to move from *learn about* to *learning*, which not only includes but also emphasizes process—not just as a route to learning but the very essence of learning itself. When a student simply *learns ab<u>out</u>* something, the information usually just goes in and then out again. It stays in just long enough for the test. But when the student is really *learn<u>ing</u>*, the information goes in and stays in. It sticks, becoming integrated through application and reflection.

For example, a student can *learn about* the craft of writing— the mechanics and conventions, organization, flow, word choice, transitions, syntax, and sentence structure. A teacher can give pointers and suggestions: write what you know; carry note cards to quickly capture ideas whenever or wherever they arise; let your writing be raw in the first draft. But *learning* to write comes from repeated applications of these principles: multiple drafts, revisions, and final edits in preparation for public consumption.

The transformation from *learn about* to *learning* requires application. If we stop at *learn about* we have short-circuited *learning.* To close the circuit and turn on *learning*, application and integration are musts. *Learn about* precedes *learning* but if it does not move forward into application and integration, it is short lived and soon forgotten.

A babysitter I hired years ago made the distinction between *learn about* and *learning* crystal clear. Jennifer, a freshman at the University of Wisconsin, was a high achiever who begrudgingly spent a year as a fashion model after high school in order to earn money for college. She did not like the modeling scene or being away from home, but she made a bundle of money.

One day, when driving her back to campus, I asked Jennifer about her classes. A test in Wisconsin geology was on her mind. "Oh, that's an interesting subject," I said. Images of the Kettle Moraine, the Dells, and the Lakeshore of Superior flashed through my mind.

She brushed me off, explaining she wasn't interested in geology—here or anywhere. "I just study for the test and when it is over, it goes out of my brain. That's the way I've always done it."

I thought, *Wow, what a waste, to say nothing of the hard-earned money she saved while modeling.* Jennifer had mastered *learn about* but did not seem to have much experience with *learning*.

The Necessity of Un-Learning

This move from *learn about* to *learning* is essential for creating and doing a Senior Capstone.

To do a Capstone, students had to unlearn dependency and passivity. They had to unlearn the notion that school is the sole place of legitimate learning. They had to unlearn that there was one right answer. They had to unlearn that learning is limited to what is quantifiable and measurable through testing. They had to unlearn that the product was more important than the process. They had to unlearn that they were not accountable for their own learning. They had to unlearn that learning is boring or is not applicable to their real lives or to the real world. They had to unlearn that they are not good at learning and that what they really want to learn is not relevant, not "school-related."

As their teacher I too had some unlearning to do. I had to unlearn that being an effective teacher is about control. I had to unlearn that I have to be right or have all the answers. I had to unlearn taking things personally. I had to unlearn that being objective is realistic. I had to unlearn that I can reach every student. I had to unlearn that learning is not limited to the classroom or school. I had to unlearn that all learning must be tied to academics. I had to unlearn that school success and life success are not equivalents.

Students of the twenty-first century must break through layers and layers of educational conditioning to reach their core, the place where their true interests and self-initiative reside—and this breaking through is a process of *unlearning*. When shifting from *learn about* to *learning*, students wake up and show up.

The Shift Is Happening

The shift from *learn about* to *learning* is happening in favor of students driving their own learning. It is a shift towards learning in the real world in real time rather than learning about it once or more removed. The shift calls upon students to be the generators of their learning rather than passive recipients of information and knowledge.

Notice the shift in language. Read down the left column below, which consists of school subjects. Then compare to the right column, the new language of learning. Which is more compelling and energizing? The shift is from a single-minded overemphasis on learning about content to a more dynamic and creative kind of *learning* that balances content with process.

English	Communication
Math	Empowerment
Social Studies	Innovation
Science	Experimentation

Over the last several years, I have had numerous conversations with high school faculty, administrators, and students about opening up education to be more relevant, real-world, and meaningful for the student. At the high school where I taught, there were numerous initiatives moving in the right direction towards greater choice and customizing education to the student: early college, dual enrollment, online learning, integration of academics with technical training, independent study, standards-based education, and of course the Senior Capstone.

More can be done. I believe, as do others, that students should be supported in customizing (with guidance) their high school education once basic requirements are met regardless of grade level. This would not only maximize the relevance and meaning for the student but also the economic value of all the money we invest in education. Given the budgetary constraints on education, the flat economy, and the dismal job market, this seems not only feasible but also desirable and wise.

Additional possibilities to those mentioned above for customizing education include: internships, service learning, travel, apprenticeships, research assistant, special institutes, certification programs, on-the-job training, entrepreneurships, school exchanges, interdisciplinary team projects, and leadership projects, to name just a few.

All the above options are evidence of the shift from passive to active students, from a prescribed to a customized curriculum, from *learn about* to *learning*. Learning in and for the twenty-first century is shifting so the student's core interests, proclivities, and aspirations are at the axis.

4

Senior Capstone

Maple Street

When you grow up in rural Maine, you have to make your own fun. Dan Voner used to mess around making films with friends. But as with all true fun, there needs to be an element of challenge, risk, or adventure. In his Capstone proposal Dan wrote, "I had made movies in the past, but they were always crazy, a little chaotic, with little or no theme. That's what inspired me to write a script this time with underlying plots, one that made sense, and then actually film the script and see how it comes out."

Through family connections, Dan was able to find a professional scriptwriter from California. Dan's mentor, Michael Caissie, advised Dan to read movie scripts that had been sold; this was the best way to see how it is done. "[Michael Caissie] told me that he learned more from reading scripts that sold than all the college courses he took about screenwriting." Dan used no notes during his Capstone presentation and spoke in an unwavering enthusiasm for over an hour about his process to create an 88-page screenplay,

Maple Street. Working with his mentor was "real deal" and it energized him. Dan felt he was rubbing shoulders with the big league, and indeed he was.

In writing the script, Dan worked with an energy and focus he had not experienced before. In his reflection paper, Dan wrote, "I have never been a very active student when it comes to academic work, but surprisingly I had no trouble pumping out an 88-page script. I learned that when I find something that interests me, I can actually do a good job with it. . . . I am much more confident in myself and my capabilities when it comes to scholastic subjects, a strength that I lacked before."[1]

When I checked in with Dan for the first time on his progress, I was both impressed and a bit baffled. He had written 45 pages. I knew Dan as first and foremost an athlete with an attitude that school is just-something-to-get-through. He was clearly bright, "cool" and charming. If I remember correctly, fellow classmates scoffed aloud when he shared his idea for his Capstone. Perhaps that is one reason he kept quiet about it. But I also suspect that he felt somewhat removed and independent of the school's resources. I didn't blame him. There was neither a film studies class nor a film club in the high school at the time. Instead, he was working with "real-world" professionals from California. His professional script reviewer, Isabel Lombard of Lucy Rocks Productions, had reviewed *Fight Club*, Dan's favorite film. In her review of *Maple Street*, Lombard wrote, ". . . the writer definitely has potential with his wild imagination, great characters, and clever dialogue." Lombard rates Dan's script *excellent* for dialogue and *good* for characters and originality. On the advice of his mentor, Michael Caissie, Dan had his script registered with the Writers Guild of America, which protects his work, as does a copyright.

Maple Street is a comedy-drama—the best-selling screenplay genre. To get started, Dan quickly wrote a brief summary of his screenplay to use as a guide. "Once this was complete a whole flood of ideas came to mind," he explained. To help him capture his creative mind at full force, his mentor had some advice. "Michael told me to make sure that I always carry a pencil and paper around with me so that whenever I get an idea I can immediately write it down. I even woke up in the middle of the night a few times and had to jot my ideas down for fear of forgetting them." Dan found out that even though he may sleep, the muse does not. This was all the evidence I needed in order to know that Dan had reached a deep level in the creative process.

When the flow started to slow down, Dan took a break for a few days and sought out the advice of friends and family on where to take his story next. His mentor cautioned Dan to watch out for too much outside influence. It was Dan's story and no one else's. *Right on,* I thought to myself. Great advice for life, too.

Other invaluable advice from Dan's mentor included: balance action and dialogue, keep the main character in all scenes, watch the pace and flow, use the three-act structure, and tighten up the story. "Every page of your script should push the story towards the inevitable ending and what you are trying to say." His mentor also acknowledged the difficulty all writers have in the middle of a story. He brought Dan into the fold. "Don't worry about that because every writer who has ever written, from myself to the great ones, has a hard time on this part." In terms of length, Caissie advised cutting the script in half, presumably to keep the project manageable and focused, given the time frame.

Caissie acknowledged Dan as a talent. "I really, really liked the beginning and the end of your script, Dan. It shows you can definitely write and that's something you either have or you don't. You do a great job of mixing the seriousness of the political strife going on in the world with the carelessness / easygoing attitude of your main characters."

Upon rereading Dan's script from five years ago, I was again struck by its complexity of plot, the existential questioning and the life wisdom embedded in the cynical and nonsensical humor of adolescent boys-to-be-men. Dan uses a kind of *Matrix*-like altered reality mixed with apocalyptic world events while his characters play poker, drink beer, watch TV, look for "hotties," banter, and jockey for the alpha social status in the hierarchy of high school, bullying included.

Eclipsing the story is a worldwide nuclear war set off by the U.S. "War on Terror."

As the world crisis escalates, Dan's cast of characters turns a deaf ear to the alarming news of pending doom coming from the TV news while they are in the midst of a poker game. "Turn that crap off! It's giving me a headache," shouts one of the players. While the "filthy rich" have a chance to buy their survival with the purchase of scarce bomb shelters, the guys prepare in their own way. Their doghouse bomb shelter is a mocking commentary on the world about to end.

The juxtaposition of humanity's insanity with the silliness and playfulness of youth is Dan's style. In the screenplay, Dan even pokes fun at the caricature of rural Mainers, of which he is one. "A news specialist shows a chart [and] points out that ... it is easy to see that with the destruction of Maine, the American Red Neck population has decreased by more than half, leaving a few hick provinces left in Alabama and Oklahoma."

As for the story line, Valnardo, the main character, dies during the nuclear fallout and finds himself in a room alone with a balding man named Host, a kind of wise teacher. Host explains, "Try to follow me. The world you have been experiencing isn't real. It's no more than a highly advanced virtual-reality, video-game, top-of-the-line technology, to be exact." Valnardo learns that he is really Mark. Valnardo is the bad-boy character Mark plays in the simulated world.

Mark asks, "Well, why would so many people live in a world that's inside of another world?"

Host answers, "Why do people live inside their television set, or on the Internet? They need an escape. Why do people pound gallon after gallon of alcohol down every week? Do you really think the idea of killing your body sounds attractive?"

Host continues. "The real world, the one we're in now, is so utterly perfect, that people can't handle it. People need imperfection. In the perfect world there is no need of food, jobs or money; there is no war, poverty, or STDs."

Host has been selected to rehabilitate the likes of Mark or those who threaten to corrupt the perfect society. "Most of them are young cocky imbeciles, much like yourself," explains Host.

Still true to his "young cocky imbecile self," Mark laments the loss of the need for food in the perfect world—"that must mean there's no fat people, I love fat people. They boost my ego when I'm down. . . . I need my freak show!"

No more evidence needed. We have witnessed Mark, as the bad-boy character Valnardo in the simulated world, passively condoning the bullying of an obese male student dubbed Mattie Moo Cow.

When Host sends Mark back to the simulated world, he is now in the body of Mattie Moo Cow and experiences bullying first hand. Meanwhile, his simulated character, Valnardo, is now played by the former Mattie Moo Cow and is shown walking arm in arm with Mark's crush. Whereas Mark playing Valnardo never got the girl because of his cocky behavior and perverted comments, the former Mattie Moo Cow who now plays Valnardo does.

When Mark returns to Host from the simulated world, he is not happy about playing Mattie Moo Cow. Host is not sympathetic, saying, "You thought lesser beings were amusing, so I let you experience how it felt. Other people's misfortunes aren't an ego boost anymore, are they? By the looks of it, he (Mattie Moo Cow) was playing the game a lot better than you were, and you can't stand this! The fact that some fat boy is so much more impressive than you are drives you insane. I'll let you in on a little secret. The key to this game is simple: All you have to do is ask yourself, 'Could somebody else be living my life better than I am?' If the answer is no, then you have nothing to worry about."

Host gives Mark one more chance. Mark returns as Valnardo to the simulated world. This time he gets the girl and welcomes Mattie Moo Cow into his group of friends. Even Host knows that *experience* is matchless for learning and growth.

Along with other faculty members, I was truly "wowed" by Dan's Capstone. Upon reflection, I never knew this was in him nor would I probably ever have known if not for *Maple Street*. I suspect Dan would not have either.

Postscript: In college, Dan Voner majored in political science and minored in history. He is now attending law school with the goal of becoming a criminal defense lawyer and ultimately a Supreme Court judge. In a recent Facebook message, Dan wrote this reflection: "Looking back, I owe a lot of my academic success to senior seminar and the Capstone project. It was the first moment in my life that I discovered education could actually be interesting. I remember everyone was very surprised, including me, that one of the school's biggest jocks decided to write a screenplay. A year later in undergrad, my screenplay fulfilled the prerequisite for a special creative writing class where every student was challenged to write a novel in one month, which I did. From there my passion for writing continued to grow, and the skills that I developed helped me to stand out with the creative essay that I wrote for my law school application."

Part II

Shift in Six

The Story of an Initiative that Stuck
&
How Students Raised the
Senior Capstone

5

Initiativitis

Education is notorious for initiatives—new programs that are expected to improve student engagement, achievement levels, and readiness for higher education. Initiatives are often short-lived, and teachers who have seen initiatives come and go give them pet names such as "the latest and greatest" and "trendy-mendy."

In the six years that I taught seniors in high school, there was at least one and sometimes more than one new initiative or focus per year. The list included: student voice, literacy, student-led conferences, laptop initiative, differentiated instruction, Good Citizens of the Month, academic support, standard-based instruction and assessment, professional learning communities, college tours, early college, and dual enrollment.

All these initiatives have merit and seek to empower students and improve the effectiveness of teaching. Some initiatives are still standing and growing, while others have lost steam. Success depends upon steady fuel injections of human energy over time. The life span of an initiative also depends on the breadth and depth of the buy-in, support, and involvement within the school and larger community.

While writing this book, I heard the echo of initiativitis in another state, community, and school district. An attorney and father of students in middle school and high school was showing me his friend's house for sale. We chatted a bit. He was clearly involved with his children's education and was knowledgeable about the issues challenging their school district. "You know, he said, there are lots of good [school] initiatives out there, but they just seem to come and go. Unless you stick with something over time, you can never really know its impact or effect. An initiative is just that, a beginning, a starting point that needs to be raised and nurtured, just like the kids."

It has been my experience that if an initiative is given enough human fuel and time to tweak and morph, it will take on a life of its own. It has also been my experience that, while it may be the adults who plant an initiative, it is the students who grow it or not.

Coming Unleashed

It was like a mantra coming from faculty who knew that I was an author. "Write the [Capstone] stories. Write the stories." After a six-year gestation, from inception to full integration of the senior initiative, I became the witness and keeper of innumerable "Capstones stories" that had had a transformational effect on seniors. To let the stories go untold would be to shortchange the unwritten "contract" I had with the seniors to illustrate the power and impact of the Capstone model for learning in the twenty-first century.

Here is how it happened—how I was unwittingly led to design and develop the senior initiative by an unleashed dog.

Shea, my beloved 80-pound collie, was the culprit. Shea had developed several tricks and techniques for getting off-leash: jump up, bite and shake the leash, mouth the hand that held the leash, slip the collar, or pull his walker with all his might. To see him run free off-leash in an open field was a sight to behold and never failed to take my breath away. He transformed into his full beauty and power. Every opportunity was taken for Shea to be unleashed.

One accidental "unleashing" had momentous significance. Shea slipped his collar after jumping out of the car for a walk in the 260-acre nature conservancy that abutted the local high school. He had picked up a scent from the school cafeteria and ran headlong across the vacant high school parking lot in hot pursuit. The straightest shot from the woods to the cafeteria's back door was between a row of "portables," or mobile structures used as extra classrooms for a crowded school. As I ran past the portables in pursuit of Shea, I caught a glimpse of geometric designs reflected off the back windows of the main high school building and onto the side of the portables.

After Shea feasted on the scent of food at the cafeteria's back door, he eased off, with nose to the ground, to meander back, on leash, to the portables so that I could inspect and contemplate the luminous circular shapes, with a four-pointed star at the center, that were lined up six-in-a-row across the siding of the portables. I commanded Shea to "Sit" and petted down his glistening golden coat in the low light of the setting sun. This bought me both the time and stillness to wonder at the reflected shapes. As I did, an inner dialogue ensued, percolating up from my core, completely out of the blue.

"You're going to work here."

"Where?"

"In one of these portables."

"You're kidding. Doing what?"

"Teaching."

"What! That is absolutely preposterous! Not going to happen . . . No Way!"

I had other plans and a new job offer since moving to the area from the Midwest. Furthermore, I had never wanted to be a teacher. I knew that way back when I was a senior in high school. I even remember my words: "I don't know what I want to be, but I know what I do *not* want to be— a teacher or nurse."

Models of Inspiration

Seemingly from nowhere, the images of my favorite high school teachers, Mrs. Johnson, Mr. Struglia, Mr. Jackson, and Mr. Starna, whom I had not thought of in years, filled my memory screen. Each of these teachers ignited a love of learning and curiosity in me that I had not felt since breaking the reading code in first grade. The love of learning and curiosity stuck. Today, I can become interested in almost anything; this turned out to be essential in my role with the Senior Capstone.

My high school teachers were as different from each other in personality and style as the subjects they taught. Mr. Struglia, the bellowing Italian, sang up and down the halls about the mighty mitochondria, the powerhouse of the cell. Sophomore English with Mrs. Johnson was an immersion into the awakened minds of the transcendentalists. Mr. Starna did not lecture at the front of the class but arranged desks in a circle and prompted his history students to think deeply and debate respectfully. Mr. Jackson transformed a motley bunch of musicians into a force of sound, precision, snap, and just the right amount of sass to become the number-one high school marching band in the state of New York.

My inner voice resumed. "These are your role models for what is now needed. Inspiration. That is your gift. That is your job— to inspire. I wondered, *Inspire whom, and for what?*

End of conversation. I walked my dog home. I refused to listen to any more inner talk about *teaching*. I turned it off and drew the line.

The Call

Shortly thereafter, a call came from the high school's director of guidance asking me to be on the Senior Year Committee. My son, a senior in high school, essentially finished his public school education during his junior year. So when the call came, I was not only willing, but had some ideas.

Leadership at the high school wanted to develop a program to make senior year more challenging, meaningful, and relevant to the eighteen-year-old young adult. The intention was to transform senior year from a fourth year of high school into a transition year preparatory for adulthood and higher education. I was invited onto the Senior Year Committee as a parent and community member. Being new to the area, I was a neutral choice. I had no history, agenda, or vendetta. What I *did* bring to the table was a passion for meaningful education.

The committee finalized the senior initiative into two components, Senior Seminar and Senior Capstone. The bigger hurdle seemed to be finding someone to lead it. An interdisciplinary approach involving the entire faculty was an essential aspect to the program; the committee did not want the senior initiative to be housed in or become the "baby" of any one discipline or academic department. The committee could not expect an established faculty member to take it on. After all, this was experimental. The committee struggled with the idea of finding someone "interdisciplinary." How would they advertise? What would be the qualifications?

During these discussions, I felt a quickening. In an attempt to help, I used myself as an example. I was a "bundle of interdisciplinary" by way of master's degree, educational philosophy, and way of life. I had a strong background in human biological sciences, as well as psychology, political science, education, and communications. I had held leadership roles in the community as an elected school commissioner for a large municipal school district and had consulted in public school systems statewide. I was a published author, professional educator, public speaker, and workshop leader. Most importantly, I thought, I was curious and loved to learn. As if reading my mind, several committee members studied me in silence over the rim of their glasses. Within a month, I was sitting before a committee of a different kind, an interdisciplinary interview committee of twelve representing all departments in the school.

Outlier

In the beginning, the Senior Initiative was a real "outlier." I borrow that term from Anne Fadiman, author of *The Spirit Catches You and You Fall Down.[1]* While speaking at the Commonwealth Honors College at UMass Amherst, Fadiman described her outlier status as a journalist writing an account of a Hmong family coping in the foreign world of Western medicine for the treatment of their child, who had a life threatening case of epilepsy. It was a story of culture clash that altered and cross-sectioned the lives of all those involved. Fadiman viewed her outlier status as an advantage that resulted in a book that is widely used to teach the importance of cultural competence in the education of health professionals.

Outlier status *can* be an advantage.

Most would agree that physical location and space represent a primitive sense of power and importance regardless of setting. In the first year, the Senior Initiative was experimental; it was not part of the main culture of the school. So, as might be expected, the program was first housed out in a portable.

The Senior Capstone was not only outside the main building, but also outside traditional education. The Capstone would shift teaching and learning from a focus on *content* to include the importance of *context*, and from a focus on *product* in terms of grades or standardized scores to include the vital importance of *process*—not just as a means to learning, but as learning itself. It would shift into the empowerment of applied learning and knowledge.

Moving In

When the portables were no longer needed after a school renovation, I became a roving teacher in the main building, moving from classroom to classroom. I worked with seniors individually in the library on their Capstone. The way the seniors related one-on-one was significantly different than in class. One-on-one, seniors tended to drop their classroom persona. I became acquainted with their more authentic selves. Seniors shared their hopes and dreams, fears and stresses. They became real and interesting people.

It was in this context that I also became more familiar with the various worlds that students lived in. I learned about their jobs, political views, lifestyles, favorite teams, bands, and films. Life rounded out. My role expanded to include mentor and advisor as students coped with the emotional roller coaster of senior year and their transition into adulthood.

Our meeting place, the library, was in the center of the school—an ideal spot for the integration of an initiative into school culture. Students passed by several times a day en route to the cafeteria and the gym. This central location made the Senior Capstone highly visible to the entire school community, not just to students but to faculty and administration as well. The location was also symbolic of the Senior Capstone as being a school-wide undertaking and helped to create interest or at least curiosity among the upcoming student population.

By the third year, the Senior Capstone had its own classroom on the first floor. This was our reward for being a bit too loud in the library and claiming more than our share of space. The assignment of a classroom was also a sign that the Senior Initiative was now "legit" and deemed to be a full-fledged program of equal standing to all other courses and programs. We were off experimental status. This had an impact on the students. Senior Capstone now had a home, a headquarters, rather than borrowed space.

Six Senior Classes Raise the Capstone Initiative

It is the educators who plant an initiative, but it is the students, ultimately, who grow and raise it with each successive class towards the final Shift into school culture.

First Shift: All-in-One Class

The first class in 2005 was the All-In-One-Class. They were a composite of all types, a kind of window on what was to come. There were resisters and "hoop-jumpers." (A hoop-jump is doing just enough to pass.) There were a few high performers and transformers. But the resisters and hoop-jumpers predominated that first year. The seniors viewed the Capstone as just more of the same, an obligation rather than an opportunity. Not until the high performers and transformers dazzled others with their Capstones did the resisters reluctantly "get it." The dazzlers of the first year set the bar high for all future seniors and demonstrated the wide-open possibilities for Capstones.

Despite their initial resistance, the personality, proclivities, and passions of the first-year seniors leaked out. The diversity of Capstone topics made the mind spin: homeopathic veterinary care, screenplay writing, legislative intern, wholistic health, art therapy, photography exhibit, canine training, car design, small business plan, auditions for college admission, interior design, geothermal heating and cooling, animation, museum exhibition, guitar design and construction, bilingual children's book, public mural design and painting, documentary filmmaking, championship weight training, gender attraction, investments, one-woman vocal and instrumental concert, stand-up comedy, sensory integration . . . all original, experiential, and applied. It is interesting to note that when given the choice, students choose to create. This was a trend with all subsequent classes.

The Senior Capstone is like a Maine spring. Winters in Maine are long and can extend up to six months from beginning to end. Spring does not emerge gradually, but seems to break out all at once as if it has been holding back and has some catching up to do. That's how it seems with the Capstone and is part of its phenomenon: the seniors break out and bloom.

Second Shift: Hold Steady Class

The second year was the time to hold steady, to catch one's breath after the launch year. It was a time to let the Capstone settle, sink in, and consolidate. The diversity of topics continued to expand: Greek mythology script-writing, the inside scope on college admissions, Meyers-Briggs Personality Types, sports medicine, operation of a small business, healing a phobia, night photography, computer construction, time travel, directing a senior class play, directing a kindergarten musical *A-Z Does It*, composing and producing Quebecois music, prevention of girl bullying, intercultural history, dance, and cuisine, analysis of children's art, creating a senior slideshow and video, newspaper reporting, anatomy and physiology of the human heart, prenatal care and natural childbirth, cosmetology, scuba diving, totem carving . . . all original, experiential, and applied. Overall, the Capstones in the second year were mostly solid. It seemed the dust had settled.

However, the audiences for the Capstone presentations were sparse, with only one or two faculty members and a couple of friends attending. Some parents came. School administrators graciously gave audience to the seniors when available. The presentations needed work. Seniors needed coaching in public speaking to do justice to their Capstones. One faculty member was adamant that the seniors deserved a more dignified, formal, and reliable space to deliver their Capstone presentation, not just any available classroom. I agreed. (It is always great to have a colleague do your advocacy work for you.)

Third Shift: The Breakthrough Class

After the catch-our-breath-year, it was time to raise the bar on the Capstone. Things changed significantly the third year. First, the Senior Capstone had its headquarters on the main floor. Seniors were grouped in small labs of 8–12 students. Each lab took on its own personality. Seniors cleverly maneuvered their schedules to get in a lab with their buddies. Seniors witnessed the unfolding progress of their peers' Capstones—positive peer pressure. They networked and supported one another.

Lab was a place to let go a bit, share, support, and dare I say, have F.U.N.—*F*undamental for *U*nderstanding and k*N*ow-how. (A tenet of brain-based learning is that fun and enjoyment enhance learning and memory.) Creativity was in the air and almost seemed contagious. Seniors wanted to shine with their Capstone rather than merely complete it. They wanted the Capstone to represent their identity and values.

This was a class of free spirits. They were not into school spirit, but their own spirit. They were neither joiners nor conformists and would not be coerced. The Capstone fit them; they made it their own rather than just accept or resist it. Many seniors voluntarily doubled the required fieldwork hours and several lost count. The Capstone topics continued to expand: solo travel, simulated *This American Life* radio program, portraiture, original rock opera, school reform, furniture-making, architectural design, novelette, chivalry, animal carvings, assertiveness training, therapeutic massage, training guidebook for track and field, politics of genetically modified food, original jazz composition, subliminal advertising and promotional art, Arabic, Mandarin, journaling and the uncensored mind, nutrition for fitness, propaganda, Prom Preview as fundraiser, addiction and the adolescent brain, Reiki, reflexology, aeronautics, therapeutic dogs, re-victimization, cross cultural study of sex education, affordable travel, Middle Eastern dance, and storytelling through art, music, and narration, to name a few . . . all original, experiential and applied.

This class was without fear. They would not comply with rules that made no sense or that offended their dignity as responsible young adults. They came and went according to their class schedules rather than school rules. They preferred the concept of an open campus and behaved accordingly. Several seniors graduated early. They were not rebelling but living according to the dictates of their own rhythms and sense of personal dignity.

This was the Breakthrough Year—the year a critical mass of seniors took hold of the Capstone. They had dropped fear. They related to faculty more as mentors and advisors rather than authorities or teachers. Respect had to be earned. They were not afraid to speak their truth and articulate their point of view.

As presenters, the "breakthrough" class took their role seriously. They moved into the school theater to accommodate larger audiences. Presentations became more colorful and multimedia. Audiences swelled in size and the theater filled in. In keeping with their nature, these seniors left classes to attend their friends' Capstones. The word got out. The desire to attend Capstone presentations trickled down to the lower grades. Teachers complained and a system had to be put in place to limit the number of Capstones that each student could attend. Parent attendance went up and so did their pride; they brought culinary treats and cameras. News of the Senior Capstone was circulating in the community.

Fourth Shift: The Promoters

The Capstone was growing up. The following year the principal decreed that all Capstone presentations would be held in the school theater. Teachers brought their classes. Students advertised their presentations by posting fliers around the school and making announcements on the PA system, posting on Facebook and even on YouTube. It was also the year that the Capping Ceremony was created. Megan was a top cross-country runner in the state. After her Capstone presentation, Megan's audience thought it fitting that she run under a human arch on her way to the Capstone Board to stamp herself "Capped." From that time forward, running under a human arch became a lasting ritual for all future Capping.

This same year, the seniors transformed a barren gymnasium into a multimedia festival complete with elaborate displays, demonstrations, music, and food samples for the First Annual Exhibition of Senior Capstones. Despite initial grumbling, seniors took it in their own hands and created an extravaganza—a real showcase for the local media. One reporter noted that the students enjoyed learning without textbooks or tests. The Senior Capstone Exhibition became a lasting tradition as well.

Fifth Shift: The Second Generation

By the fifth year, the Capstone had passed through an entire high school generation of four years. The fifth year was the Second Generation class. Over a quarter of the fifth-year class had older siblings who had been in one of the four earlier classes. Seniors continued to choose original topics for their Capstones: groupthink and mob mentality, the female brain, *The Wizard of Oz* as an American icon, medical terminology, the Maine fishing industry, indoor toxins, the relativity of beauty, surveying, technological detection of paranormal phenomena, the use of fear by governments to control society, travel above the Arctic Circle to study Inuit language and culture, sea glass art, modern shamanism, dune buggy construction, the highly sensitive person, beekeeping, small-plane and hot-air-balloon pilot's license, raising awareness of and fundraising for alopecia areata, jazz and gospel music composition, helping to draft and lobby for legislation on autism, to name a few. . . .

Changing topics among the Second Generation seniors was rampant as they tried various possibilities on for size and fit. These seniors understood that their topic choice must be of high interest, with staying power over six months. Hoop-jumps were out. Change of topic was not only allowed but also expected as part of the process. The Second Generation seniors did not settle but insisted on doing what was meaningful to them, whether tracking a moose or piloting a hot-air balloon. They really "got" the whole Capstone, the whole process from inception to completion.

Sixth Shift: The Collaborators

By the sixth year, the Capstone had become an integral part of the school culture. It survived budget cuts and was no longer experimental. By its very presence, the Capstone generated more choice, experiential and applied learning across the curriculum. Support from the students, administration, parents, and community steadily increased.

The greatest shift occurred among the seniors themselves. The size and scope of their Capstones continued to expand. An increasing number of seniors wanted their Capstone to inform, to be visible, and to have a positive impact on their community. To do so, they needed each other. Creators in the twenty-first century value teamwork and collaboration. Interdependence is valued over independence and increases the F.U.N. factor.

In the Collaborator Class, nine pairs formed. Approval for pairs was based on the determination that the Capstone could not be done by one alone; the roles and division of labor must be clearly defined. The pair had to be compatible, with complementary rather than overlapping skills. Three of the pairs pulled in many more members of the senior class and student body as needed for their Capstones: a one-act play entitled *To Cure a Nation*; a school-wide music video entitled *Lip Dup*; and a fundraiser for The Patrick Dempsey Cancer Center for Hope and Healing entitled *Seniors Got Talent*.

This shift towards collaboration was highly significant. When the Capstone program first began, all seniors were required to do individual projects. But when seniors designed Capstones of greater scope involving more work, collaboration became a necessity. The seniors were showing the ways of the twenty first century.

The Final Shift: Insider

In early spring of the sixth year, I had the somewhat unnerving experience of watching myself conference with a student while I was in a kind of disembodied state. Surprised, I thought at the time, *Oh, this is what I used to do*. It felt like the shedding of a role I had worn close to the skin.

Another sign of the final shift was when a senior pair chose to choreograph a music video backwards. It made me recall my initial meeting with the school superintendent when he said, "You will impact education in the district backwards." I intuited his meaning, but still asked him what *he* meant. "Well, when we start a new initiative, we usually start at the other end and build forward. You are starting at the endpoint. The effect of the Capstone will move backwards." I gulped. That sounded like a tall order.

Then there was Beth's Capstone on dream analysis. One day in class, Beth asked to collect classmates' dreams for the purpose of practicing dream analysis under the guidance of her mentor, a Jungian dream analyst.

I shared a dream of a bonfire in my backyard attended by 15-20 alumni representing all six classes. We each sat on our own rock in a circle around the fire, sharing and swapping items on our Life List.

Upon hearing my dream, a senior "googled" the symbolism for circle. "It means completion," he said from the back of the room. "Uh-huh," I said. *Coming full circle—the process of creating from inception to completion.*

I was ready to move on. I felt fulfilled and had other items on my Life List, this book being one of them. The Capstone was secure and would continue on.

This was further confirmed when an entering freshman came up to me and said, "I know what I want to do for my Senior Capstone."

"Really?" I marveled. "What is your idea?"

"I want to learn about homelessness by being homeless myself for a time." The superintendent had been right in his prediction after all—the Capstone had reached backwards. It had trickled down into the middle school. Marvelous.

At the other end of the high school spectrum, a usually reticent senior raised strong objection over a proposed change in the Senior Capstone Board. "I've been waiting four whole years to see my name up there and I want it just like it has always been. It's a tradition."

And then there was the perspective of an alumnus soon to be a senior in college. Rachel, at home during summer break, offered to help me pack before moving. The two of us chatted freely as we wrapped pictures and dishes. She was the first person I trusted to tell about my plan to write this book. Her reaction was both supportive and enthusiastic. "The Senior Capstone was the first time in high school that students had to take ownership for their learning. That's what made it so hard. We were so accustomed to just letting the teacher do it. It really raised the bar and wasn't always pretty. It changed the whole game. It was *really* empowering though."

As I packed to leave one life and move onto another, I reflected how the *Shift in Six* was a walk between two worlds in education. Rachel was right—it wasn't always pretty and certainly not easy. But nevertheless, shift does happen and it *needs* to happen. The right shift can be a real game changer.

6

Senior Capstone

Sojourn

Hanna wanted to go across the pond. Since she was ten years old, London had been her dream destination. Hanna held onto her dream for eight years. When she got older she worked and saved money. Then she saw her chance—the Capstone. It would not be a trip, but a test. This was not the kind of test that could be written on paper. It would be a journey of a lifetime, a "coming of age" rite of passage. For Hanna, the journey must have the romance and intrigue of a foreign land, across the ocean, on another continent, and in a world-class city she had never seen before. Most of all, it had to be taken alone. Going solo was the essential part of the test.

I felt both a charge of excitement and a pang of fear when Hanna proposed a solo journey for her Capstone. Hanna referred to her solo journey as a *sojourn* in order to create an old world mystique around it and to deflect any suggestion that she was merely traveling for her Capstone. The sojourn was her chance to extricate from peers, school, and family, and be alone with Hanna. It was a time to go inward and think about her future without interruption and to refresh and awaken her senses in a foreign land.

Wow! A dream Capstone—something the senior always wanted to do but never had the chance, excuse, permission, or support to do. I could barely contain myself. What better use of a Capstone than to fulfill a dream? I had no idea that Hanna had such a dream, nor did I have a clue that she had the nerve to follow through. Foreign travel was not common for students living in rural Maine. I had students who were not familiar with the city of Portland, less than an hour away, nor Boston, only two and a half hours away.

For starters, I ran a quick feasibility study on Hanna's idea for her Capstone. First up was the preliminary clearance question. "Do you have your parents' approval?" (The parent consent form was signed and I spoke with her father for verification.) "Do you have the resources?" (She had a job and was saving.) "Have you traveled abroad before? (Once, on a school trip.) Why alone?" I even went into "mother mode," feeling protective and issuing caution. "You are a beautiful young woman; there are safety issues here."

Hanna took great pleasure in my uneasiness. She had been successful in rattling me. She delighted in dangling her Capstone in front of my face just to see the reaction again. What power!

Who to get for a mentor? I knew plenty of people who travel abroad to far-flung countries and continents, but I did not know any solo travelers, least of all young women. I was really stumped. This rattled me even more because I had a knack for helping seniors find mentors—against the odds in a rural community in central Maine—but this time I was at a loss. Even an all-district e-mail produced nothing.

Hanna playfully teased me, "Well, without a mentor, I guess I won't be able to go, but if I do, I won't meet the requirement for a mentor and you'll have to fail me." Now her tease felt somewhat mocking. Hanna continued to press. "A high school senior successfully travels abroad for ten days alone and comes back to talk about it but she fails her Capstone because the requirements were not met. Sounds like a news story to me," Hanna chided. Other students joined in the fun and warned, "If anything happens to Hanna on her "sooojourrrn," that will be it for the Capstone, Mrs. Aronson—over and out!"

We found secondary sources on solo travel but that is not the same as talking with someone who could answer questions and share their experience. Finally, Hanna found the solution herself—travel blogs for women who travel solo. There were many good suggestions that for the most part were common sense. The consensus amongst the bloggers was that traveling solo in Northern Europe was safe for women. Feeling at risk or in danger was rare. Solo travel isn't for everyone, the bloggers admitted. You have to be able to feel okay with not feeling okay all of the time.

The tip most emphasized by the bloggers was to know your destination thoroughly and familiarize yourself with the lay of the land and its customs. The bloggers had other suggestions too. Make contacts before arrival and leave a daily itinerary with someone back home with copies of all travel plans, tickets, schedules, and passport. Be polite but cautious with strangers, and set boundaries as needed. Do not look like a tourist. Quiz the hotel staff for advice about places to avoid. My favorite response to Hanna's queries to the bloggers read, "Wow, a senior project on sojourning? Why didn't I get cool assignments like this when I was in high school?"

While Hanna found all the street-smart suggestions helpful in planning her trip, she was particularly keen to hear about the advantages of solo travel that she was to experience herself. As Hanna would later write in her Capstone paper, "You meet more people than if traveling with a companion and you are in control of your schedule and activities—you do not have to compromise. [You] go where you want, when you want, for as long as you want, or not."

Luckily, a member of the faculty had been to London numerous times and was able to share travel books, maps, and brochures to help Hanna select sites to visit and become familiar with the city of London. Now Hanna's dream destination seemed closer and more real, all within the familiar surroundings of school. Hanna's confidence was on the rise.

Hanna's biggest fear of traveling solo was not being alone per se or being without companionship; it was her fear that other people would stare at her (especially in restaurants) and wonder why she was alone. Of course, this makes sense for a young adult who is at the height of social sensitivity. To remedy this fear, Hanna followed the advice in travel guides. Before embarking on her sojourn, she practiced going to public places alone and watched closely to see who was looking at her—usually no one. This helped alleviate her anxiety about being noticed or sticking out.

After three months of researching, planning, and arranging, spring break finally came and it was time for Hanna to fly to London on her ten-day sojourn. She made a detailed itinerary for each day,

> ... knowing full well that I wouldn't follow it on my trip, but use it as a sense of comfort. The itinerary will act as a sense of direction, should I find myself looking for something to do. . . . I expect to go through ups and downs during the trip, but to overall end up with an experience of a lifetime. *The journey of a lifetime is one that many plan, but few actually go on.*

After arriving in Heathrow Airport, Hanna took the Tube but did not arrive at Westbourne Park until ten at night, requiring her to find the Tria Hotel in the dark. She went down several wrong streets and thought she was lost. A bit rattled but secure, she finally got her bearings despite the dark and found the hotel. Hanna wrote about her disorientation upon arrival. "On my first night in London, I kept thinking, 'What am I doing here?' I was trying to comprehend the enormous reality of what I had done. I had taken a plane from the United States to England by myself, to spend a week traveling around alone. The idea was now reality; it was hard to comprehend."

Hanna followed her packed itinerary quite closely and ventured out one day to Salisbury, Stonehenge, and Bath. She added a day in Paris that was not in her original plan. She saw Notre Dame, the Eiffel Tower, and the Louvre. Paris ended up being her favorite part of the whole trip. Surprisingly, despite her longtime dream of visiting London, it was actually Paris, the City of Light, that most captivated her. Hanna's eyes lit up when she spoke of her day in Paris. Could this be one of those life lessons—that, to our surprise, it is the unanticipated turn on the way to our planned destination that holds the richness of our experience?

On her return home, Hanna had all the physical evidence of her journey: photos, travel stubs, motel bills, brochures, and trinkets for memorabilia. Smart girl. (All seniors must show the evidence of their fieldwork. Hanna had one of the more exotic collections.) In addition, Hanna came home with some jewels in her crown that can only come from experience:

> I found that being by myself allowed me to do more. I met people that I wouldn't have. . . . I did what I wanted to and when I wanted to. I also found that I was able to simply soak up my surroundings because I wasn't busy talking about gossip back at home or current events. I was living in the here and now.

> I found that you are not only learning about the new environment that you are seeing, you are learning about yourself.

> I learned that being on your own isn't always comfortable, but that I can handle it. I learned a lot about who I am and who I want to be. Sojourning

gave me lots of time to think during a time of big change in my life.

*I learned that whatever happens in life, I now know I'll be okay.

I will remember my sojourn for the rest of my life. It has opened the door for future travels and hopefully will open a door of encouragement for other people as well.

At Hanna's Capstone presentation, the principal expressed great admiration for all the research and planning she had put into her Capstone. He was most impressed with her courage to carry it out and even envied her time to think in solitude, without interruption.

It was evident that Hanna *did* have the journey of her lifetime, thus far. In a world-class city across the pond, Hanna learned some invaluable life lessons that she never would have learned in the classroom. She learned that it's okay to not feel okay some of the time, but that, whatever happens in life, she knows she'll be okay. Hanna pulled off her dream and passed her own test. I wondered, *If she hadn't been traveling solo would she have ever reached the City of Light?*

Postscript: Hanna is pursuing a bachelor's degree in business with a concentration in tourism and hospitality.

Part III

Full Circle Learning
at Full Capacity

The Capstone Model
&
Components

7

The Capstone Model & Components

Words of the Wise

We have all heard the famous words of Confucius: I hear, I know. I see, I remember. I do, I understand. What is less known is what Confucius told his students: "I want you to be everything that is you, deep at the center of your being."[1]

That is what the Capstone tries to reach—the center or core of a student's being. To learn on the sidelines may feel safe, but it is usually half-hearted and yields only mediocre results. When you're on the sidelines, something is missing: the connection with one's self. Youth is the time and opportunity to tap into the core, to get on track with one's purpose. In the words of Osho Zen Ta, "You are not accidental, existence needs you. Without you, something will be missing in existence and nobody can replace it."[2]

At its best, education should be the path to the core of one's self. "Education is to draw forth, not impose upon."[3]

The Capstone can be a means to tap into and draw forth the best in students found at their center or core. The Capstone model is not meant to be a panacea, the latest and greatest, a new fad or trend, but rather one model for learning that fits the creative idea age of the twenty-first century and this generation of students.

The Capstone Model

This chapter illustrates the Capstone as a model for full-circle learning through which the student creates to learn and learns to create. The Capstone model has been under the radar but is becoming more visible today at both secondary and higher education levels and is a graduation requirement in many schools on both levels.

It can also be used as a model for students in middle school, high school, or higher education seeking to design their own educational and learning experiences in the form of self-designed and self-directed study.

The point is not necessarily to replicate the Capstone per se but to emulate the spirit of its model for full-circle learning at whatever level or context so students are empowered to learn at full capacity.

"So What Is a Capstone?"

That is the first question I ask my students.

Students "google" *capstone* and read the synonyms aloud: "apex, crowning achievement, peak, pinnacle, height, climax, sum, crest."[4]

"That's the idea," I say in my teacher persona.

In architectural terms, a capstone is the top stone of an architectural arch. An arch marks a transition, an initiation, a doorway or gateway from one level to another.[5] Numerous colleges have an arch under which incoming students enter and graduating students exit.

"So a *Senior* Capstone represents the peak," I tell them, "the summit of your education K–12 and the passage from one stage of life to another and from one world to another.

"To come full circle, let's look at where you started." I close the classroom door and continue . . . .

Hardwired to Learn

"When you were very young, in the first five years of life, you had an internal drive to learn that only stopped when you were sleeping. You were hardwired to learn. Your rate of growth was exponential. Think about it: you learned to walk and talk in just two years. The complexity of those two skills alone is astounding. By age five, you could run, jump, skip, throw and kick a ball, sing, dance, draw, write, build, play, and pretend. You started asking incessant questions by age three and hopefully you never stopped. Your vocabulary increased daily and hopefully never stopped. Some of you started 'reading' by age five and hopefully never stopped." This last statement triggers some chuckling around the room.

I continue with a story of the beloved University of Vermont graduate school professor, Betty Boller, who was wholistic and interdisciplinary in her approach to education. One day she posed a question to the class of doctoral students: "After the age of five, the learning rate slows down and the curve levels off. Why?" Members of the class responded with explanations that expounded upon theories of cognitive and human development. (This was in the days before imaging technology and the explosion of information on brain development.) Our beloved professor extraordinaire just smiled and listened. When the explanations ran out, Professor Boller said, "You are all thinking way too hard. It can be explained in just one word that starts with the letter *S*." No one said a word. No one dared. Finally a brave soul offered, "School?" That was it. Despite the decades between then and now, I have never forgotten that day in class.

Up to age five, learning is child-driven. Upon entering school, a child encounters a prescribed and required curriculum

⸏nated sequence traditionally favoring logical and ⸏uistic intelligences. This leaves other intelligences (visual/spatial, bodily/kinesthetic, musical/rhythmical, naturalist, existentialist, intrapersonal, and interpersonal, as identified by Howard Gardner, author of *Multiple Intelligences*) underserved. The child is no longer driven from within and in time will become a passive recipient rather than active seeker.

Falling Out of Love with Learning

It is a travesty and tragedy when students fall out of love with learning. Yet so many do. In the world of school, good grades and high test scores measure success, rather than creativity, innovation, and original thinking. If a student does not find meaning in or is not motivated by grades or scores, he may take his learning elsewhere where it is safe.

For example, Tom did his Capstone on wildlife photography. He eagerly shared his new batch of photos with his classmates after each trip to the North Woods in search of robust wildlife. When sharing his photos, Tom rose to a new level of poise and confidence. It was readily apparent that he loved photography. I asked Tom once what it was about photography that hooked him. "Because," he said, "no one can tell me a photo is wrong." Tom went on to explain, "I have been told all through school that I was wrong." But not with photography. Within the safety of photography, Tom dared to experiment with technique. He sought challenge and saw a different view of himself through the lens of his camera.

Choice

With the Capstone, the student decides the curriculum, both content and context. So I tell my students, "That is where you begin, with choice. What are you most interested in? What are you curious about? What is your bend? What is your proclivity?" Jokingly, I tell the seniors that the only restriction on the Capstone is that it has to be legal. Since students have so little practice in choosing their learning, and because they are conditioned to think in terms of school subjects, the door needs to be opened up to a wide array of possibilities and categories for students to consider:

- Dream: always wanted to do/learn/create but needed an excuse to do it
- In-depth and/or original research on a specific topic/issue
- New skill, or existing skill developed to another level or on a different trajectory
- Community service
- Design, construct, create
- Teach, mentor
- Self-improvement or personal growth
- Career choice

I continue: "It is your birthright to learn—what, how, where, and with whom, all without limits. You are here to learn, not solely in school, but in life. School does not contain the whole content or context of your learning—your life does. It is your greatest teacher." This may sound revolutionary but I consider it evolutionary.

As I emphasize repeatedly with my seniors, the Capstone is full-circle learning from inception to completion: the process of creating. The components listed below move in concert, merging and spiraling and integrating in progression towards an apex or final point:

Capstone Components:

1. Choice of topic
2. Pre-Search and Research

3. Proposal
4. Mentor
5. Fieldwork/Applied learning
6. Capstone Paper
7. Portfolio
8. Presentation
9. Capping
10. Reflection.

A senior once told me, "I did not really know what you meant by 'full-circle learning' even though you showed a visual diagram and gave us examples. It was not until I actually finished the Capstone myself did I really get it." This is quite a common experience for the seniors and why they need to complete all the components and keep moving through the process even though they do not always "get it" until finished. Admittedly, there is often grumbling along the way.

Making a choice shifts the learner from a passive, reactive-responsive orientation to the active orientation of creating. Choosing a topic is the hardest part of the Capstone but over time the students recognize this as the key.

Choice of Safety, Choice of Challenge

In the first several years of the Capstone, seniors tended to make safe choices choosing topics they already knew about, identified with, had a skill in, or felt were relatively low risk.

A critical number of seniors did break away and made a choice that stretched them in some way, got them out of their comfort zone and into their core, reaching untapped potential just waiting to be put to use. Zack, a senior in the first-year All-in-One Class, was such a student. Zack made a choice that was both transformational for himself and the Capstone. He led and showed the way. I place Zack's story here to illustrate how the

Capstone components mix and merge, spiraling towards the apex of completion.

Zack to the Rescue

Zack aspired to be a professional graphic web designer and as a high school senior was already skilled in this area. He even had his own design company. In the introduction of his Capstone paper, Zack described how he could have played it safe by using his existing skills and knowledge:

> So I had to make a decision, should I take the easy way out, or should I dig a little deeper, and actually get something from this [Capstone] project. I made the decision that every teacher and adult in my life hoped I would. I decided to build a guitar . . ..

Zack's interest in the art of guitar making was spawned through playing the instrument since middle school. "I was completely ignorant of all woodworking skills and the facts about different woods, so I decided it would be a great idea to start a project that would be challenging and interesting."

Zack's mentor had a successful business as a custom guitar designer and maker. With the help of his mentor, Zack designed and built his own mahogany, Telecaster-style custom guitar, a commitment of 100 hours. It was a work of art, a real beauty. Zack entitled his Capstone "The Beauty of Playing Your Own Creation."

Zack and his mentor made an equal exchange of knowledge and skill. Zack designed two possible websites for his mentor's guitar-making business. In reference to his mentor, Zack wrote, "Neither of us could have predicted our compatibility, or the capabilities we could offer each other."

Zack truly rose to the challenge. His Capstone did not go unnoticed by the faculty or student body. It became a model for future Capstones in terms of getting outside one's comfort zone and going for the learning stretch. Zack dared to be a beginner. He did not fear what he did not yet know. He approached his Capstone with an attitude of interest and openness by seeking challenge over safety, and creativity over convention.

Zack's project was clearly "cool" and easily showcased. It served to ignite the imagination of future seniors for the endless possibilities inherent in the Capstone. Zack did not concern himself with a grade. "I didn't want to do something just to get the grade." Nor did he limit himself to basic requirements. "I knew what I was proposing to do was far beyond the set of guidelines for this project, but I also knew I would walk away with something I would never forget." (Zack did six times the amount of required fieldwork hours.)

Zack stayed clear of group mentality when making his choice. He was independent of mind; he chose to see the Capstone as an opportunity rather than obstacle. As Zack wrote in his reflection paper, "I was surrounded with the endless drone of complaints . . . and despite all of the complaints and moans, Senior Capstone is an excellent idea. It is a great opportunity, and I can't imagine if I hadn't had this opportunity."

Increasingly over the years it became clear that the choice of topic is of paramount importance. Seniors want to choose a topic that highlights their interests or do something unique and unexpected. For some, showcasing is an important factor. Above all, it must not be boring or "lame" to themselves or to others.

It is not unusual for students to try several different topics on for size before settling on one. This is encouraged and viewed as part of the process. Students have limited experience with making choices and decisions. Choosing a topic is a learning stretch and experience in itself. Once the seniors find their match and they commit to it, momentum starts to build and they are off. If a senior never really explores ideas or options but passively lets someone else or circumstances such as time force a decision, then each step is a struggle.

It is thrilling to take a Capstone choice that is not strictly "academic" and transform it into an empowering and metaphoric learning experience, such as learning the art of pottery in order to shape one's life by one's own hands rather than being shaped by the hands of others, or learning photography as a means to see the world from a different angle with greater beauty and dimension, or learning to play and perform bass guitar as a means to becoming visible on the stage of life, or learning to fly an airplane to reach greater heights and see the "big picture."

So the choice is theirs—choose safety or choose challenge. Safety runs the risk of feeling like "more of the same"—and challenge holds the potential for transformation.

Where in the World? Pre-Search and Research

Once the student makes a topic choice, pre-search comes next. This is an exploratory stage to help scope out and more finely tune the Capstone. During this stage, a "working" or guiding question is formulated. It must be open ended and investigated with an open mind. There is no one right answer but multiple possibilities.

The truth of the matter is that students balk at research. Seniors want to go straight to fieldwork, the experiential component of the Capstone. They also balk because research is associated with writing a research paper rather than having value in itself. Research is best undertaken with a spirit of a hunt, looking beyond common knowledge to make a discovery. Curiosity is required. "The more I learn, the more I want to know." That is why it is called *re-search*.

Because students tend to center their Capstone on fieldwork or the experiential component, they are often not exactly clear about what to "research" for their chosen topic. For example, Ryan built a private road to a previously inaccessible pond on family land for his Capstone. He surveyed the area, designed the road, and operated heavy equipment in its construction. He might have researched soil erosion or computer technology as related to surveying. But neither technology nor soil was his passion. However, he was interested in roads, and the story behind the U.S. Interstate Highway System piqued his interest. He conducted research on the development of highways across the United States and soon uncovered the fascinating history of how the auto industry lobbied the federal government to develop the Interstate Highway System, turning the United States into a one-person-one-car society. Locations fed by the Interstate Highway System boomed and those that were bypassed withered away. Through his research, Ryan learned the power and significance of roads, from opening up access to a pond in the woods to opening up and connecting an entire country.

In a similar vein, two seniors working together as a pair chose the challenge of breaking the Guinness World Record for the tallest sugar-cube tower but were stymied as to what to research. *What was there to research about sugar-cube towers, they wondered?* I suggested researching *The Guinness Book of World Records* itself—the history, the categories, the application process, the verification of records, the longest-held records, and the biographies of the keepers themselves. The results of their research not only turned out to be very interesting but also had a significant impact on their motivation. The pair learned that *The Guinness Book of World Records* is the most widely purchased book after the Bible. They learned that the record keepers were most often regular people, not unlike themselves. This energized them and bolstered their confidence into believing they might actually be able to break the tower record.

Contact with Ashrita Furman, the holder of 100 different world records, was a huge boost for their Capstone. Furman helped them believe in themselves and the real possibility of breaking the record—and after multiple designs and many fallen towers, they came within an inch and a half of doing so.

When asked why they chose their particular topic, they answered, "Because once you break a record, your name is in the Guinness Book forever. You go down in history."

It is always satisfying when a senior does research, develops a position, and then "goes into the field" and changes his point of view. Eric did his research on wind power, which he supported as a source of green energy. Eric attended a statehouse hearing on the subject and heard the arguments of both proponents and opponents of wind power. But when he visited the proposed installation sites offshore from coastal Maine islands, he saw for himself how the windmills would compromise ocean views. His family had a camp on a coastal island. When he learned that the islanders would not even benefit from the electricity generated by the wind power, Eric altered his position; the push for wind power, he decided, should be slowed down.

Sometimes students are tempted to toss their topic when they come up short on sources for research. Jared wanted to make a real tree *house* for his Capstone—a livable structure that was weatherproof, complete with frame, roof, windows, and door. But at the time of his research, sources on tree houses seemed very limited and were primarily focused on construction of the backyard version. Jared needed to broaden his search beyond what he could find at the school library. His trip to the state library, within a few miles from the school, turned out to be fruitful. There he found hot-off-the-press, glossy, full-colored books on tree houses from around the world. His widened search opened up Jared's view of the tree house: it is by no means just a kid's thing but in fact had become a worldwide state-of-the-art green alternative to the second home—a getaway, studio, private workplace, guesthouse, and resort.

Sometimes it is the fieldwork that ignites the student's curiosity to do research on their topic. Research and fieldwork often run side by side and cross-fertilize each other. For example, Melissa thought she would give yoga a try. In the beginning, she was sufficiently interested, but not really committed. Her mentor taught not only poses and breathing techniques but also the philosophy behind yoga—living a balanced life of mind, body, and spirit. Melissa was intrigued. She loved both the physical activity of yoga and its philosophy. As her experience with yoga deepened, she made the connection between the two. This motivated her to research yoga further, learning the teachings as well as the movements. At her presentation, Melissa not only demonstrated yoga but also shared its philosophy with equal enthusiasm.

Some students designed and conducted original and empirical research for their Capstones, using the scientific method. Examples of original research included: the correlation of role with the phenomenon of groupthink, the effects of classical music on test performance, the correlation between the weight of backpacks and back strain, the effects of massage and reflexology on stress levels, and the rating of attributes relative to the concept of beauty, to name just a few.

As shown by the examples above, research is not a linear process with finite beginning and end points. Rather, research is an ongoing process combining primary and secondary sources with direct experience. In many cases, it was the experiential component of the Capstone that drove research. Direct experience is what gets students interested in their topic to begin with and then leads to a desire to learn and research more with the effect of seeing their Capstone topic in a wider context. Research is a natural way to learn, explore, discover, make new connections, and find solutions to unanswered questions. It comes naturally when it's chosen rather than forced. Research is not limited to a formal academic core, but is an aspect of everyday living. Research is what everyone does when there is a need to know, learn, and grow.

The Magic of Mentors

Research helps seniors find and connect with community mentors. But due to their fear of rejection and a lack of communication skills, seniors are often very reluctant to seek out and make initial contact with a potential mentor. To the seniors' surprise (but not to mine), community members are not only willing but also eager to mentor high school seniors. They are flattered that a young adult chose them to be a mentor. Those who are passionate about their field or special interest usually love to share and pass it on. Rarely was a senior turned down.

When the Capstone program was still new, it took some convincing for seniors to understand the value of a mentor prior to obtaining one. "Mentors are gold mines for research sources," I said. "They share their networks as well. Mentors can help you focus your Capstone to fit the six-month time frame. A mentor's role is to guide, advise, and support you. They want you to succeed and will stick with you during your Capstone process. However, they will not hold your hand or do the work for you. Mentors are the best judge of your accomplishments and can vouch for your growth and new learning. They also give recommendations and may help get you a job."

By this time, seniors get the idea that mentors are another key to the Capstone. It is just a matter of finding one.

Finding a Mentor

"How do we find a mentor?" they asked, as if looking for a four-leaf clover in a ten-acre field.

"No one in Maine builds dune buggies," lamented one student.

"How about animation? Where am I going to get a mentor for that?"

"I want to learn Mandarin. Where in *Maine* do I find a mentor for Mandarin?"

"What about Arabic?"

"Who can mentor me about chivalry?"

"Fashion blogging?"

"Propaganda?"

"Biomimicry?"

"Quantum biofeedback?"

"Handwriting analysis?"

"*The Wizard of Oz* as an American Icon?"

"Car Design?"

How and where to find a mentor? Some seniors are tempted to abandon their first-choice topic because they cannot imagine that there is anyone in rural Maine who can serve as a mentor on their topic.

I advise, "Use your resources. Start to network with those you know. Do not eliminate your choice of Capstone because of the challenge of finding a mentor. Mentors can be found in many places. They do not have to be in person. We've had mentors from California, Colorado, Florida, Alaska, Massachusetts, Washington, D.C., and New York. You need not be limited by location. We live in a global society—use e-mail, social networks, cell phones, or Skype."

Mentors and Community Building

What thrilled me the most was community members serving as mentors. In some cases, school parents mentored seniors. One school parent, a local artist, was a mentor for a senior painting a mural. Another school parent, a local musician, became the mentor for the artist's son. The wife of the artist mentored a senior in Middle Eastern dance. The father of an alumnus was the mentor for Zack, the student mentioned earlier who built a custom-made guitar. Other alumni mentored seniors for real estate, investing, coaching, acting, creative writing, and filmmaking. Community mentors help get the word around town about the Capstone.

Mentors who are retired particularly enjoy the companionship of youth and can share not only their expertise, knowledge, and skills but also their wisdom. The Capstone has brought together generations that otherwise might have no way to connect. For several seniors, the Capstone provided a way to reunite with an estranged parent. These seniors deliberately chose a topic with the hope that it would interest and thus involve their estranged parent. The bait worked: through the Capstone their parents reentered their lives.

It is not unusual for the student to mentor the mentor in some way. In the case of Amy, she wanted to learn how to run a small business. Her mentor's photography business was struggling in the weak economy. Amy developed a new business plan for her mentor.

Mentoring as Mutual

The mentoring relationship is different from that of authority figures in seniors' lives such as teachers, parents, coaches, or employers. A mentor advises and guides but lets the student run the show and learn from her own experience. The mentee can take or leave his mentor's advice. The mentoring relationship is by mutual agreement; there is no obligation. Either party can discontinue if it is not a match or there is a lack of rapport, commitment, or benefit. The mentoring relationship requires a level of maturity, communication skills, and commitment that challenge many seniors.

The Mark of a Mentor

Great mentors make for great Capstones. Those Capstones that go beyond what either the senior or others believe possible have the mark of a mentor. For example, Matt drew 80 original drawings for a multimedia story sequence. His mentor had taught at several prestigious arts schools and was able to provide a level of support and guidance hard to match.

Mentors can literally take seniors where it would be risky without them, such as winter camping in a handmade quinzee, or snow hut, in the North Woods of Maine, or scuba diving for underwater photography in the cold waters of the Atlantic, or hiking 100 miles on the Appalachian Trail.

Mentors also open doors and give access to the community, such as the state legislature, various state agencies, local businesses, health practices, police departments, and community theaters.

In sum, the process of finding a mentor and establishing a relationship with one is a learning stretch in itself and a useful lifelong skill. The mentor-mentee relationship is mutual. That aspect alone sets mentors apart from authority figures. Mentors can expand the seniors' networks and open doors to unknown opportunities. Perhaps best of all, mentors can become adult friends and support systems as seniors step into their adult lives.

Making and Framing It Up: The Proposal

Once seniors choose their topic, do preliminary research, find a mentor, develop a guiding question, and scope their Capstone, they are then ready to write their proposal. Once their proposals are complete and have been approved, the seniors can proceed with their Capstone.

The proposal, a working document, provides a framework, plan, and direction for the Capstone. It maps out clear beginning and end points. The proposal is a contract of one or two pages signed and dated by the senior. In the proposal, seniors rate their level of interest for their topic, name the type of Capstone (see Choice), discuss prior knowledge and experience with their topic, and describe the area(s) of challenge and degree of learning stretch.

In addition, seniors analyze how their Capstone is a "perfect match and seamless fit" for their learning styles, multiple intelligences, and preferred learning environment. What is the guiding question to drive research, investigation, and new learning? What will they do for fieldwork? What is their plan of action and their time line? What do they expect as a final outcome? What are the mentor's credentials and contact information? How is their chosen topic current or cutting-edge? How does it reflect the rapidly changing world? Finally, how will their Capstone enrich the community in some way?

Finally, how will the execution of their Capstones exemplify twenty-first-century skills: risk taking, applied learning and real-world application, self-direction and executive functioning, innovation and creativity, effective communication and collaboration, and literacy in technology and information?

Their Favorite Part: Fieldwork

Invariably, seniors center their Capstones on fieldwork, or what they are planning to *do*. Fieldwork is the experiential or applied-knowledge component. It is the students' favorite part—the *heart* of the Capstone. Fieldwork is the real deal; it is tangible and visible and provides lots of latitude to learn and create in a much wider arena than within the confines of a classroom. Fieldwork provides elbowroom for trial and error, experimentation, and modification without constant oversight. Making mistakes is not only okay but also expected as part of the learning process. Lowering the fear of failure raises the willingness to take risks.

When doing fieldwork, students learn to cope and rise above the unexpected but inevitable trials. Fieldwork requires problem solving as well as creative and critical thinking. It requires the courage, initiative, and confidence to ask for advice, assistance, or resources as needed. It is the chance to be a beginner in a longed-for-but-never-had-the-chance-to-do interest or to step out as a leader in an area of highly developed knowledge and skill.

Fieldwork is the centerpiece and showcase of the Capstone. It is in fieldwork where seniors feel the power of their innovative and creative minds, where they feel the joy of self-expression, where they can see tangible progress and results, where they can experience anew their birthright—the inherent drive to learn and create. When the fieldwork takes hold and I feel the electrical charge, I just stand back and let the students go.

A member of the sixth year class wrote, "Fieldwork is an important part of taking ownership of education because as I said earlier, planning something and actually *doing* something are very different things. We have spent years and years learning to plan things and looking at examples. We are finally doing something, manifesting our plans into product, and it's nice to see."

With the Capstone, seniors are finally out of school and into the world. Their mentor becomes the primary person they relate to for learning and creating. As seniors get out in the community and become visible and valued sources of youthful energy and vitality, they receive positive feedback, applause, and recognition they were not expecting. It is as if a link in the chain has been added to the community, making it stronger and more whole.

Rating of Research and Fieldwork

So how do the seniors rate research and fieldwork? The feedback collected in the first three years was narrative and in the last three, numeric. (I realize that to separate research and fieldwork is arbitrary, for the two are intricately connected.

This is not meant to be scientific research nor statistical analysis, but rather an indicator or snapshot of how students view two different but related approaches to learning.)

Question: "To what degree do you value fieldwork/ research as a learning tool on a 1–10 scale, with 10 being the highest?"
> The Class of 2010 rated fieldwork at a mean of 9.2 and research at 8.5.
> The Class of 2009 rated fieldwork 9.1 and research 8.5.
> The Class of 2008 rated fieldwork 9.4 and research 8.7.

The narrative reflections from the Classes of 2005–2007 expressed a similar rating of fieldwork and research with fieldwork consistently rated higher than research.

It is interesting that the difference in the spread between fieldwork and research is fairly consistent but not widely separated, less than one point in a range from 1 to 10. This suggests that the students regard research and fieldwork as closely related as indeed they are. I would even suggest that fieldwork had a positive effect on student attitude towards research. Fieldwork helped raise the relevance level and value of research.

In the first three years of the Capstone, the minimal requirement for fieldwork hours was 15 with a range of 12–100 hours. Three years later, the minimum requirement was increased to 30 hours, the mean number of hours the preceding class had voluntarily devoted to fieldwork. In that same year, the building of an automosextacycle (6 seat- cycle) and a 12-foot wooden dinghy took 200 hours each, doubling the previous record of fieldwork hours that had been logged.

Community Service with the Capstone

A notable number of seniors create Capstones that support their wider community in ways that are meaningful to them as they take on the roles of leaders, role models, and creators. Examples of Capstones that were in service to their community include: writing original scripts and directing youth in one-act plays; creating with youth a bilingual children's book; drafting legislative recommendations with an advocacy council in support of treatment for those with autism and testifying before a legislative committee; co-leading workshops on the balance of power and prevention of abuse in relationships; creating and organizing fun-filled fundraising events to support nonprofits; mentoring a foster child; organizing and conducting sports clinics; and coaching middle school basketball and soccer teams.

One pair of seniors found, to their surprise, that volunteering in the community is not easy. The intent of their Capstone was to identify the various ways youth could volunteer and give back to their community. When working with social service, youth, or health organizations, volunteers receive the same screening as employees, which include personal interviews, references, and security checks. This can be time-consuming and discouraging to youth who just want to help. They feel that they are held suspect when asked in interviews why they would want to volunteer. In their research, this Capstone pair found that "community service" has a negative reputation and is associated with restitution for a crime. That is, those who do "community service" have been ordered to do so by a court of law. It is imposed upon the "volunteer." Whereas, with the Capstone, service to the community is chosen. The opportunity is created and carried through by the student.

In sum, fieldwork is the students' favorite part of the Capstone. It always makes my heart sing when students ask at the beginning of the school year, "When can we start our Capstone?" I understand that they mean the fieldwork.

Thinking at the End of Your Pen: The Capstone Paper

It is practically unanimous among students: The research paper is daunting and a drag. Academic formatting. Synthesize, analyze, and don't plagiarize. No amount of coaching or cajoling seems to lift the gloom.

Some students struggle to write eight pages of original work. From the teacher's side of the desk, writing research papers is preparatory for higher education. On the students' side of the desk, writing a research paper is meaningless toil, just another hoop-jump in order to graduate.

To try and buck up the dreaded research paper somehow and punch some meaning into it, I plant a few images and ideas: "Writing is thinking at the end of your pen, or your fingers on the keyboard. Find out what is known out there in the wide world about your topic. Write meat, not fluff to fill the page. Be in your paper; write in your own voice. Above all, don't bore your reader or even worse, yourself." Throughout the Capstone process, I always advise seniors to use their resources when the going gets rough.

Well, that last piece of advice—use your resources—they like best of all. And so they do. I suspect that a few papers are in large part the work of girlfriends, and in some cases, mothers. Some Capstone papers get major overhauls by older siblings home from college. And admittedly, some get major revision and editing from me so the students can graduate.

The real stinger comes when seniors are reluctant to share their research findings during the Capstone presentations. When I asked them why, they reply, "I don't want to bore my audience." Boring the audience is the worst offense and their worst fear, beyond the jitters of public speaking. That was telling. Whatever was in those research papers was boring—dead words on a page, just there to meet the requirement. There was no sense of connection with the rest of the Capstone.

Students experience traditional modes of research as passive, in contrast to fieldwork, which is an active form of research.

So rather than fight, argue, persuade, or cajole, I align with my students. "Research papers are dreadful; they are the worst. Pity me who has to read them! It is painful; they are so boring, dead, and dull. And most of all, a waste of time for both of us!" To further illustrate my point, the seniors and I volley a bit:

Me: When you finish writing a research paper, what happens to it?

Students: We hand it in.

Me: Then what?

Students: The teacher grades it.

Me: Then what?

Students: We get it back.

Me: And then?

Students: We throw it out.

Me: Tossed?

Students: Yep.

I rant a bit more. "What a waste of time and energy for it to travel such a limited route and with such a short life. All that research and writing and only one person other than the writer gets the goods!"

So to remedy the situation, the research paper got a major makeover. It had to be explicitly sewn into the whole, to be an integral and essential part of the Capstone. Out with the research paper and in with the Capstone Paper, a synthesis of research and fieldwork. Finally a paper with purpose.

I explain. "The purpose of the Capstone Paper is preparatory for your Capstone presentation. It is your outline. Your research sets a context for your Capstone. By sharing cutting-edge information about your topic, you'll grab the attention of your audience.

"For example, what is the happiest country in the world and why (according to studies of positive psychology)? Can self-hypnosis improve athletic performance? Why are bees dying and what is the implication for agriculture?

"Write only what you are willing and eager to tell, what you find interesting, and above all, do not be boring."

Voilà! Two hits in one: Capstone paper and preparation for the presentation. Connection accomplished.

In case you are interested, Iceland was the happiest country in the world in 2008. Self-hypnosis can improve the consistency of an athlete's best performance. Relocation and transportation of beehives are one cause of the demise of bees.

"Cap-Ready" Final Assessment

Seniors are expected to be "Cap-Ready" prior to their final presentation. (See "Capping" Ceremony.) The Capstone Paper, Fieldwork Report, and Portfolio must meet the standards and be approved. The senior is to rehearse his presentation in Capstone lab and received feedback, suggestions, and approval.

The Capstone program is designed so the senior has both independence and ongoing support and assistance as needed throughout the process. Prior to starting the Capstone, seniors receive standards and rubrics for all components of the Capstone including: the Proposal, the Capstone Paper, the Fieldwork Report, the Portfolio, and the Presentation. On a regular basis, seniors write progress reports as self-assessments and for receiving feedback and planning next steps. If necessary, special support or interventions are put in place to help the senior keep moving forward.

Throughout the Capstone process, seniors gather evidence of learning that will be the contents of their Portfolio including all formal documents, papers, and products of fieldwork (photos, video, data, drafts, drawings, all original work). In the sixth year, the Portfolio was uploaded to the Internet.

After all components have met the standards and are satisfactorily completed including the presentation, seniors write a reflection paper on their process, learning and growth. This is also their opportunity to give feedback and make any suggestions for the Capstone program.

The Capstone is "fail-proof." All students pass *when*, not *if*, the standards and requirements are met. Students have multiple opportunities to upgrade and revise work as needed throughout the process. It is not expected that the final results of the Capstones will always match the predicted outcomes in the initial proposals. Capstones tend to take on a life of their own and go in directions that the seniors cannot anticipate at the beginning. Many times, students surprise themselves and exceed their own expected outcomes.

The *time* of completion and meeting the standards on all components depend on the scope of the Capstone and the student's own pace. Some seniors need the whole school year to complete their Capstone, most finish in six months, and a few go-getters in three months. There is always the perennial senior who takes it right up to graduation. The *timing* of completion is much less important than the breadth and depth of learning and growth.

Capstone Presentations

The purpose of the Capstone presentation is much more than an exercise in oral communication and public speaking: it is the opportunity for the seniors to share their new learning in an area of strong interest, and by doing so, to broaden the world and to deepen the lives of their audience.

The presentation is where the transformation of both the student and the Capstone program itself is most evident. Capstone presentations are public affairs and became increasingly so in each successive year. Seniors step into the role of teacher or an expert on their Capstone topic before an audience of students, faculty, administration, family, mentors, and interested community members. It takes lots of coaching for the seniors to shift out of the student-report mode and step into a more confident presenter mode.

Overcoming Stage Fright

Understandably, the presentation was the aspect of the Capstone that was initially most intimidating to students. The high school did not have a public-speaking course or curriculum per se. Practice in public speaking was limited. Individual or group presentations were required or optional in only a few classes. So public-speaking skills varied widely among the students.

Seniors who are verbal in class or who perform on the field or on the stage have a basic level of comfort when in front of an audience. But even these extroverts, athletes, and actors make it clear that going solo is vastly different from being in a class, on a team, or in a cast.

Over the six years, the general sense about the presentation grew from trepidation to celebration. Moving presentations from empty classrooms and into the school theater had many advantages. It helped the seniors step out of their student role. The theater had versatility. Lighting and sound could be controlled. The setup could be arranged to maximize the confidence of the presenter: either standing behind the lectern, in front of a large screen, or taking over the entire stage for displays, demonstrations, or performances.

Surprisingly, despite the initial reluctance, seniors came to feel more comfortable presenting in the theater than in a classroom. Sharing the stage with a wide screen diffused the pressure of a solo act. Being on stage set them apart from their audience. The darkened theater helped the presenting seniors focus and maintain composure since they could not see faces in the audience.

In the first several years of the Capstone, PowerPoint was heavily used—a safe choice. As confidence and creativity grew, Capstone presentations became more representative of the multimedia generation. Seniors used video, music, recordings, digital images, voice-over, and much less text. Going multimedia increased the comfort and confidence level of many students. They felt in their element displaying their techie and media prowess.

Present Yourself!

"What is your most important visual?" I ask. Pause. *"You!* Present Yourself!" Capstone presenters were expected to dress for success. "The presentation is not just on the screen but also in your attire. Dress like it is the most important interview of your life," I suggested. When the seniors trade their T-shirts and jeans for khakis, skirts, ties, and jackets, they morph into adult speakers.

What's Your Point?

Presenters are encouraged to engage the audience as much as possible—to make their Capstone presentations interactive. They are coached to highlight the cutting edge aspects of their Capstone—what is beyond common knowledge—and to develop their presentations around a central *Point.*

For example, the central *Point* of a Capstone on domestic abuse is that it happens across the socioeconomic and cultural spectrum. No one is immune, no one ever deserves abuse and there are no excuses for it, ever.

The *Point* of a Capstone on hair straightening among black women is that they spend a fortune on hair products to feel more accepted, attractive, and employable in the mainstream white culture at the cost of food, rent, and other necessities of life.

The *Point* of a Capstone on the Federal Reserve is that, unbeknownst to most Americans, an unofficial branch of our government wields enormous economic power over every citizen.

Presentation Popularity

For some seniors, just getting through the presentation by following the guidelines is a triumph, while others hold a packed house in the palm of their hand. The length of presentations varies from fifteen minutes to a full hour. There are always those surprises when seniors emerge from their shell and own the stage. Jack was one such student. His Capstone topic was on YouTube when it was new and still a novelty. He fretted about the presentation all through the Capstone process and even tried to bow out of it. Yet YouTube had turned into Jack's passion—almost an obsession. Once on stage, Jack let go and delivered an equally informative and entertaining presentation. It was real YouTube material.

Over time, the Capstone presentation became increasingly popular both within the school and with community members. Seniors started advertising their Capstone presentations with flyers displayed in hallways and on doors, special invitations were sent to parents, and the schedule was sent to all faculty and posted for the student body. Teachers brought their classes. The average audience size increased from a handful in the first year to 25 by year six, ranging from 10 to 200-plus, with all sizes in between. Most heartening was the number of parents. In the first year, only a few parents attended. By the sixth year, most parents took time off from work to attend. Seniors scheduled their presentation so their parent(s) could be there including evenings. In addition, seniors invited their friends, faculty and administrators, mentors, grandparents, aunts and uncles, neighbors, siblings, and alumni.

Capping Ceremony

"Getting Capped" is the grand finale of the Capstone and a highlight of the senior year. "Getting Capped" is short for being honored in the Capstone ceremony that takes place immediately after a senior's Capstone presentation. Once the signal is given that a senior is "Cap-ready" at the end of her presentation, members of the audience fall over each other racing to the Capstone Board for the formal "Capping." The Capstone Board is in the main entrance, right outside the principal's office. The display is always gold and red, symbolic of putting a bright idea into action.

Seniors look for their 3-inch by 8-inch gold-paper "plaque" on the Board that they stamp "Capped" as part of the Capstone Ceremony. But first, they must run under the human arch formed by two lines of friends and family who press palms together overhead to create a tunnel that ends at the Capstone Board. Running under a human arch originated with the "Capping" of a star runner. Her audience spontaneously formed an arch of overhead out-stretched arms. That was it. The human arch stuck and became part of all future "Cappings."

The meaning of the Capstone Ceremony heightened over the years as it grew to include the Capstone Board, the human arch, Capped T-shirt, and proud parents snapping pictures of their successful senior with friends, teachers, principal, and family members. It is high fives with friends and hugs with faculty and family. It is the seniors' moment, their time to shine, to bask in the adoration of family and friends, to let go and open up to the mixed feelings of relief, pride, joy, and sometimes even euphoria in accomplishing something they were not sure they could do. It is stepping into a bigger self with greater confidence and sense of empowerment.

The Capping Ceremony ritual is a powerful one. It is imbued and charged with both public and personal meaning. Passing under an arch signifies that a person is moving from one stage of life to another, a rite of passage witnessed and celebrated within community.

Reflections of Capped Seniors

Reflection is an essential component of the Capstone. It is coming full circle, tying together the two ends of the Capstone, from inception to completion. It is the awareness and acknowledgment of the empowerment and transformational change that makes it all worthwhile in the end, despite the bumps and bruises along the way.

I concluded a presentation to the State Commissioner of Education's special committee on secondary education with senior reflections. I turned off the lights and invited the thirty stakeholders in the room in turn to read aloud the words of the seniors. After a two-hour presentation, it was the words of the seniors themselves that made the greatest impact. It was then that I felt that the members of the committee really "got it."

Here are a few senior reflections. All are direct quotes:

I enjoyed being in control of my own learning. I had the choice as to what I wanted to learn and how I wanted to do it. It was also a learning stretch. I have never had that opportunity before . . .. It pushed me to go out on a limb and be in control of my own learning.

— Heidi

I learned who I really am. This project enabled me to learn about my culture as well as teach many others. I know my ancestors would be proud of me teaching children about our culture. That is what I am most proud of.

— Brian

I learned a lot about the profession [dental hygiene] I will be going into. I will be able to use my 15 hours of fieldwork towards the required 20 hours needed for college in the fall.

— Chelsey

I learned that law enforcement is what I really want to do as a career.

— Will

The Capstone project really prepared me for college . . .. I won't be so intimidated when it comes next fall. I also think that it would be really cool if I could get involved with a mentoring program again, so I could be a positive role model for young girls.

— Jamie

I loved the feeling of being able to start something so huge, and complete it so wonderfully. I have never worked so hard on something, been so frustrated on something and so proud of myself, all on the same project. The Capstone is something I could never forget, and something I will always look back on as a job well done.

— Julie

I chose aviation because I had never been in a plane before and I was curious as to what was involved in operating one. I was genuinely interested in the topic and was eager to absorb any amount of information possible.

— Mike

My greatest strength was my ability to think outside the box with my interest in the topic of time travel.

— Michael

I learned that I can be dependable and that I can do anything if I take a chance and go out on a limb. It has unleashed portions of me that I never knew existed.

— David

I don't consider any part of the project inadequate. I believe that it took a great deal of courage to do, and with a project like this, you can't go about it halfway.

— Kayla

This project wasn't something I wanted to pass, but I wanted to pass with flying colors. I wanted to prove that I could do anything.

— Will

I am not afraid of my voice anymore.

— Tyler

I learned that I am determined to become a pilot.

— Andrew

I need to step out of my comfort zone if I want to achieve my goals. I achieved more than expected in my proposal.

— Katie

I learned I could do some of the things I thought I never would do.

— Chris

I learned that I have empathy for the homeless and can make a difference. I am proud that I actually touched people with the knowledge that I have from doing the Capstone.

— Jess

When I care about something, I need it to be perfect.

— Erin

I can do anything I set my mind to.

— Hannah

I learned that I can work very hard on something if I'm very interested.

— Mike

In the end, this project was meaningful for me because I have been in love with reading since I was a very young child. For me to create a children's book is, in a way, a loop back around to where my education started, with my father reading me children's books before I was even born.

— Danica

Advice for Future Seniors

Try something that people say can't be done and do it.

— Michael

Get 110 percent involved in what you are doing.

— Adam

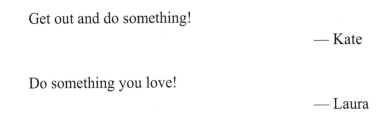

Get out and do something!

— Kate

Do something you love!

— Laura

Administration of the Senior Capstone

In the context of the current pedagogical shift towards student-centered, interdisciplinary, and experiential education, the Senior Capstone is an exemplar. It is a model for learning that is complete in itself. It traverses the whole learning cycle. It combines knowledge-based with applied learning and requires students to synthesize, integrate, and reflect on their new learning at a depth necessary to formally share with others. The Senior Capstone is successful because it provides structure and upholds standards while accommodating a wide spectrum of students' interests and capacities.

Coordination and Facilitation

A coordinator is a must for the successful administration, ongoing development, and continuation of a Senior Capstone program. The role of the coordinator is multifaceted interfacing with both the school and wider community.

An existing member of the faculty can assume the role of coordinator with adequate training, guidance, and release of workload. The coordinator's academic background is not as important as the ability to embrace, fully and confidently, the self-designed, interdisciplinary, and experiential approach to education that is the centerpiece of the Senior Capstone. The coordinator develops and specifies the components and requirements of the Senior Capstone.

The coordinator must champion the Senior Capstone and serve as its face both within the school and in the community. It is important that the coordinator enjoy a high level of communication and interaction with a wide diversity of students, parents, professionals, and mentors. Just as the Senior Capstone requires a high level of personal, oral, and written communication skills for seniors, so too for the coordinator. The coordinator orients juniors, seniors, faculty, parents, and mentors to the Senior Capstone through presentations, trainings, and ongoing personal communication and is the "go to" person with any questions about the Senior Capstone.

Helping seniors find a mentor is an essential role for the coordinator. The search for and work with mentors takes the Senior Capstone out into the community and brings the community into the school.

It is also the coordinator's role to coordinate faculty and mentor feedback, review, and final assessment of the Capstones and organize senior presentations, exhibitions, and community celebrations. The coordinator is in a position to obtain feedback from seniors about the Capstone that can be invaluable in making changes for the future.

Facilitation of the Capstones is ongoing through student interface with the Capstone coordinator, mentors, and faculty on a weekly, monthly, and as-needed basis. Seniors in *Unleashed to Learn* met weekly in small Capstone labs of 6-12 students. During labs the seniors reviewed the Capstone standards and rubrics, studied exemplar Capstones of their predecessors, worked on their own Capstone, reported on their progress, received feedback and guidance, and rehearsed their presentation. The labs became mini-communities of mutual support and engendered a sense of common identity and camaraderie amongst the seniors. Pairs formed for larger projects. Labs also served as positive peer pressure as the go-getters spurred on the slow-to-starters.

Very strong support from the school administration is essential to launch and develop the Senior Capstone to the point that it becomes fully integrated into the school culture. Change often creates resistance both inside and outside the existing school culture.

Assessment

One hallmark of the Senior Capstone is that seniors are guided through the full-circle learning process and assessed by a combination of educators, mentors, and administrators. This enriches the input, feedback, and guidance for the students as well as shares the responsibility of assessment among members of the school and larger community.

Senior Capstone graduation requirements must meet standards set forth by the school district and state department of education. The standards for performance on the Capstone emphasize written and oral communication skills and can align with the Common Core Learning Standards. Other related standards include: ability to apply knowledge, research skills, higher level thinking, creativity and innovation, application of technology, work habits and ethics, personal growth and social responsibility to name a few.

Another hallmark of the Senior Capstone is that it is an authentic assessment of the students' abilities and capacities. The student can choose through a variety of mediums and negotiate *how* they will show evidence of new learning to meet the requirements and standards. As stated earlier, the final assessments of the seniors' Capstones are the shared responsibility of the coordinator, faculty, mentors, and school administrators.

The Capstone as a Standout

The shared facilitation of Senior Capstones both within the school and out in the community and the authentic assessment of students' abilities and capacities make the Capstone a standout in education. It is the combination of the student-centered, interdisciplinary, and experiential approach to education together with the shared facilitation and authentic assessment that makes the Senior Capstone an exemplar in education that is a fit for students of the twenty-first century.

8

Senior Capstone

Digging for DNA

Charles always came to Senior Seminar late with his hood up and his long hair covering half his face. He sat slouched at his desk as if to conceal himself even more. He was tersely respectful, as if controlling himself to be otherwise. His golden-brown eyes looked wild on occasion, as if unsure he was on safe ground. The classroom routine was somewhat new for him. Charles had been in an alternative program where he could receive one-on-one instruction and tutoring. The other seniors in the class let him be and that seemed to be fine with him.

When it came time to divide the class into smaller Capstone labs, I thought Charles might bolt. And try he did. But there was nowhere to hide. He felt exposed, sitting at the long table with the other students. Over time, he tried being absent but got called on that. He requested working on an individual basis. No deal. He would miss the peer support and community building, a vital component of the Capstone. He asked to be in a different group of students more like himself.

Charles was in a lab with strong students; no doubt he felt somewhat intimidated and might have believed he didn't belong.

Actually, Charles was in exactly the right group. He had nothing to fear. His classmates were comfortable in their own skin, with nothing to prove. It was part of their nature to be respectful to all. When Charles opened up enough to share his idea of family genealogy for his Capstone, the class sounded their approval. "Cool." "Awesome." "Hey, why didn't I think of that?" one student wondered aloud.

As it turned out, Charles sat directly across the long table from James, who was an equal blend of cool and kind. One morning when James was rolling in wit, Charles finally let go. James broke through Charles' typical scowl. Charles flashed James his first smile. It seemed an ironic twist of fate that both James and Charles received Capstone awards that year.

In his Reflection Paper, Charles wrote:

> School has always been a struggle for me. It's never been a pleasant place for me to be. I guess you could say that when I'm in school, I feel like I'm in a box and I can't get out. I've made school a box that my box doesn't fit comfortably inside of because it just isn't right. I never feel free to be myself or to let anyone see me—including myself, choosing to stay safely in my box. When my classmates see my senior class picture, many will see me for the first time without a hooded sweatshirt or jacket covering much of my face. They may ask, "Who is this guy and why haven't we seen him before?" This is the real question even for me. "Who is Charles? Does he really want to get out of his box and what will it mean for Charles when he does?" This is the question that is the center of my Capstone project and motivated my research. Who am I and what am I here for?

There was keen interest within his family of their possible relation to the Merchant Prince of Boston, a highly successful businessman and philanthropist of the early nineteenth century. A river island near the township where Charles lived bore the same name at one time.

Charles decided he would investigate this mystery. Charles found from his research that his alleged ancestors were colorful characters who hobnobbed with the Founding Fathers and were major contributors of Boston's treasures: the Boston Athenaeum, the Boston Museum of Fine Arts, McLean Hospital, and Perkins School for the Blind.

Charles particularly identified with the son of the Merchant Prince of Boston. The son was an angry, wild, rebellious character who was expelled from private prep schools and failed at the businesses his father created for him. Only when he met a beauty from Maine and married did he then settle down and become successful in life. His bride's family had a home on the aforementioned river island that would later bear his name.

Charles' investigation of his genealogy was a search for a new view of himself and his family—he was digging for DNA. Charles would be the first member of his family to graduate from high school. If the ancestral connection could be made, it would have a profound effect on his self-image. But the genealogical link was never conclusive, due to records lost in fires and a family genealogy that had mysteriously disappeared. Blood link or not, though, Charles became acquainted and identified with a historical figure who had summered on a river island near his home, one who bore his surname and who started life with a temperament and attitude similar to Charles' but who ended up successful, respected, and revered in later life. DNA or not, Charles took a fresh look at his own life and the future it might hold, possibilities he never considered before.

The search for his genealogy and a link to the Merchant Prince of Boston opened up worlds to Charles that he never would have stepped into otherwise. For the first time in his life, Charles read several books all the way through. He worked with the town office, interviewed the town historian, and looked through primary records. He went to the river island and found the site of his alleged ancestor's summer home, which had burned long ago.

At the time of Charles' presentation, his mentor wrote this reflection:

> He has learned much in this journey . . . and the growth I've seen in him as the fruit of his efforts is amazing. The final product was not conclusive, but the process and journey taken to the finish were life changing and immeasurable in terms of personal effect on his own life. This was a journey he was reluctant to make and wanted to avoid if at all possible. Yet, he faced his fear and overcame all his internal objections. . . . Considering [Charles'] school history . . . this product is miraculous. He began this process virtually a non-reader and certainly not a writer in any sense of academic achievement.

Interestingly, having a mentor made all the difference. Otherwise, Charles did not think he would have passed the Capstone. In his reflection paper Charles wrote, "the school should have a lot more projects in every grade such as this project. This is by far one of the best projects I'll ever do."

Never could I have imagined that a transformation would ensue from digging for DNA. Just as the son of the Merchant Prince of Boston eventually found success in life after a rocky start, so did Charles. Despite the uncertainty of any direct line of genealogical relation, there is an undeniable connection, whether in the DNA and genes or in name and place. In the end, the source doesn't really matter. It was the family lore and mystery, the possibility that drove the investigation, the ownership of the Capstone, and, most important, a new sense of self. Epigenetics at its best.

Just to witness Charles' transformation was worth all six years.

Postscript: Charles graduated from high school and works for the town where he did research for his Capstone. Charles is responsible for the maintenance of town and elementary school buildings and grounds, the recycling center, and the community garden.

Part IV

Power at the Core

What It Takes to Create a Capstone

I always found it interesting that performance on the Capstone did not directly correlate with the level of academic achievement at either the top or the bottom of the class. Often, the seniors who took the bigger risk, learning stretch, and outcome on their Capstones were ranked in the middle of their class academically, and some were below.

Students at the top had learned to play the academic game. As one valedictorian said, "We know how to play to the judge." Another valedictorian said of the top students: "We knew how to exploit the teachers."

But the Capstone changed the game. I received more questions from students at the top of the class about "getting it right" or "doing it right" than from any other group. Also, it was this group that most often asked me to assess their work: "Do you like it?" "Do you think it's good?" I always fired back, "What you think? It's your baby."

By design, privately issued grades were not the motivator for performance on the Capstone. The rewards were both intrinsic and extrinsic: intrinsic in terms of personal empowerment and self-fulfillment, and extrinsic in terms of community witness and celebration of success and completion.

Students who raised the bar on the Capstone, who went for it, who took on the biggest learning stretch, and grew the most, all had something in common. It was not until I was writing this book that I fully understood the power source I sensed in these go-getters. It was coming from their center—their core. You could just feel it—the atmosphere filled with energy when they shared their Capstone plan or progress.

Even before I knew his name, one real go-getter ran into my classroom on the first day of school and rolled out before me a scroll of his drawn-to-scale design for a custom-made guitar. Students much preferred to show what they were *doing*, their evidence of learning, rather than *talk* about it. For example, one student came to Capstone lab eager to show the video of him flying a plane for the first time. Another student showed off the website he had created for teen employment that resulted in him finding a job after months of fruitless search.

Sometimes students wanted to save the full impact of their Capstone until it was completed such as in the opening of a photography exhibit at the local café or the launch of a handcrafted wooden 12-foot dinghy in Rockport Harbor.

Students get a real charge when the tables turn and they become the teacher, sharing their new learning—how Internet hackers work, or how to set up a mobile server, or how the Federal Reserve wields autonomous power, or how subversive messages are imbedded in advertising, or how the intricacies of the female brain work, or how the timeless standards for beauty are related to the survival of the species.

So what is the source of this charged energy? As mentioned in the introduction, there is an intelligence associated with the gastrointestinal system that is referred to as the enteric nervous system, the "gut brain," or the "second brain," the term coined by Michael Gershon, chair of the anatomy and cell biology department at Columbia University and author of a book entitled *The Second Brain*.[1]

The enteric nervous system is a neural network or plexus consisting of 100 million neurons; the connections between the first brain in the head and second brain in the gut are strong and communication between them ongoing. The gut is now considered the first line of defense of the immune system. Biochemicals critical to the functioning of the brain, such as serotonin and endorphins, are found in abundance in the gut as well. This neural network between the bottom of the sternum and the top of the navel is considered the powerhouse of the body, also known as the "core." It harnesses and directs energy for personal power and will.

By no coincidence, the core is thought to activate during adolescence. Bull's-eye! Students need to employ their core to do a Capstone—an opportunity to use their powerhouse for positive purpose. In so doing, they become empowered themselves.

The attributes of this core energy center, when in balance, correlate positively with performance on the Capstone:

- Will, personal power over self, not others
- Energetic vitality
- Taking action
- Willingness to take on a challenge
- Ego-identity; daring to be an individual
- Confidence, optimism, and enthusiasm
- Self-responsibility, self-control, and setting healthy boundaries

Seniors with a strong core took on the Capstone challenge readily. Once they settled on their topic and gathered the resources, they were off. The Capstones that thrilled me the most, though, were the ones whereby I witnessed the powering up of the student's core. One such student, who admittedly always deferred to her boyfriend, wanted to start making her own decisions and choices. She used her Capstone to study and apply the practices of assertive training and decision-making in order to pursue interests she had never allowed herself, such as join the school dance team, exercise regularly at the local fitness center, and learn ceramic arts at an artist studio. To finance these interests, she got a job and even negotiated payment plans at the studio. She transformed herself from a quiet, submissive girl into a much more confident young woman with a fuller presence and dynamic energy.

In order for the core to function as the powerhouse of the body, it needs proper feeding and exercise. Eat complex, slow-burning carbohydrates and protein every 2–3 hours to keep blood sugar levels steady. Limit sugar and caffeine. Exercise 30 minutes every day for strength and tone. Oxygenate with deep breathing. Strengthen abdominal muscles by yoga, Pilates, martial arts, or calisthenics exercises. Belly laugh. Hula hoop. Dance.

Balance is the key. Those with an underdeveloped core tend to view themselves as victims or doormats. They may be passive-aggressive or apathetic, with little will and low self-esteem. Shame shuts down the core.

Those with an overactive core may have inflated egos or an attitude of entitlement; they may engage in power plays such as bullying, abuse, or harassment. Or they may be self-centered, obsessive compulsive, or a perfectionist.

Those with a healthy, balanced core are proactive, self-directed, controlled, and responsive rather than reactive, all essential for full-capacity learning and creating.

A strong core can be life saving, as two senior girls learned from their Capstone research on women's self-defense. Women who train in self-defense are less likely to be victims of an aggressor—not because of self-defense technique per se, but because they give off a vibe and aura of self-confidence that says, "Don't mess with me." Perpetrators seek out victims who they sense are vulnerable, lacking in self-confidence. Training in self-defense acts as a repellant to the perpetrator and as a protective shield for the woman.

A healthy, balanced core is the source of empowerment of self, not power over others. It is being sovereign and self-confident with the will to follow through on the decisions and planning essential for undertaking a Capstone or any other creative enterprise.

What can a teacher, parent, mentor, or coach do to help youth activate or balance this vital power center? First and foremost, be a healthy model. Offer the adolescent choices so they practice decision-making and follow-through. Challenge them to build a positive self-image and a sense of capability through experiences of success. And last but not least, loan out your own will if necessary, enabling them to take their next steps. Be a presence; hold the space. If all else fails, get out the jumper cables.

It takes some degree of personal power and will to do a Capstone through to the point of completion. The use of power for a positive purpose undoubtedly empowers students. The essence of education, at its core, is empowerment.

Part V

Unleashed to Learn
Creating a Capstone

Senior Capstone Stories
The Heart of the Book

9

Senior Capstone

The Diamond

"Leave a legacy!" "Step up as leaders!" "Make your mark!" This was the challenge I posed to seniors for their Capstone.

When I made my pitch, the room quieted. No one stirred. They knew I was calling them out. It was just before the big game, just before they ran out onto the field of life. Seniors had prepared eleven years for this, with lots of hard work and practice.

"What do you love, what can put your heart and soul into?" I asked. "Choose a project that you *want* to do, that you can freely give yourself to. Do not do your Capstone from the sense of obligation, but from choice."

Both youth and adults learn as much or more from doing their chosen activities as they learn from "doing school." When engaged in a chosen activity, learning happens simply by way of total engagement and propulsion forward. It is not being pushed from behind but rather pulled forward by interests, desires, motivation, and curiosity . . ..

So it was with Chris. When thinking about his Capstone, he wanted to do something that was meaningful, perhaps career related. He was solid in his goal of architectural engineering for a career. He took drafting at the regional technical center and had already been accepted into the competitive architectural engineering program at a community college.

Then, of course, there was baseball, his absolute passion since playing T-ball at the age of five. Chris had blossomed early in high school, getting on the varsity baseball team as a sophomore and winning a coveted award as a junior. Like many baseball players in their youth, he fantasized about playing in the Majors some day, but he became realistic as he grew older. Still, Chris looked all-American. He was tall, fit, broad-shouldered, and had a full body smile.

When thinking about his Capstone topic, Chris spent a lot of time in the library, pouring over books with big, glossy pictures of pro baseball stadiums. He turned the pages slowly, looking back and forth between them. The glossy pages reflected onto his face. He was in another world, out of the library and onto the field. Through his eyes I came to see the beauty of what he saw in those aerial photos—the *diamond.* In Chris' eyes, the diamond field within a stadium setting was the crown jewel of architectural engineering.

Seeing his interest in baseball, I asked if he would consider the possibility of coaching for his Capstone. Not interested. Chris was smart enough to know that playing and coaching are distant cousins. Moving off of baseball and onto architecture, I asked, "Do you have any ideas for design?" No, no ideas there. I sensed that a design alone would not satisfy Chris unless he could actually build it.

After several weeks of wallowing, the breakthrough happened. Chris had obliviously driven by his Capstone on his way to school all fall. One morning, it finally hit him. The neighborhood baseball park, not far from where Chris lived, had become dormant from neglect over a ten-year period. Once a Little League field, it now looked like an abandoned, overgrown lot. The last generation that used it had grown and gone. A new generation of youth did not even know that the field existed. In a flash, Chris saw it. The diamond. He had his Capstone, or rather it had him. Chris would be the one to restore the field and uncover the diamond.

To start the restoration, Chris had to obtain permission. This venturing out into the "real world," out of the confines of school, was intimidating. Finally, Chris overcame his resistance. His first stop was the town clerk's office. There Chris learned that the field was owned by the neighborhood Community Club. The president of the club gave Chris both the go ahead and her full support. She thought it was a great idea. Chris researched the history of the field and found it dated back to 1962. The field had been used for Little League, local barbecues, auctions, and summer recreation.

When spring came, Chris was somewhat daunted by the work ahead and what he had committed himself to. The time involved would be significant. His window was narrow, from the time the snow melted and the ground dried, in mid-to late April, until his Capstone due date on May 30. He felt it might be more than he could handle with his own baseball season upon him. When he expressed his doubts in an effort to pull out of the project, I refused to listen. "This is perfect for you. It combines your passion for baseball and puts you in the ballpark of your future aspirations. Don't get cold feet now; the ground is warming up. Spring is on the way. Think of your vision for this project: young boys walking down to their neighborhood baseball field to practice and play. This is a chance to leave your legacy."

Seeing that I would not let him back down, Chris finally warmed up and he got to work. He researched the dimensions of an official Little League baseball field. He then proceeded to outline the baselines with spray paint. "With the bright orange lines on the grass you could now almost picture a baseball field coming alive again," he wrote. He had the picture, his vision.

He was on it. He was in the game. His contract was signed, not on paper but with the field and neighborhood boys.

Once he dug in with his shovel, he broke ground on his Capstone and had to see it through. The task ahead seemed daunting and time was short. Chris needed physical help but also wanted companionship so as not to have to work alone. Rather than rounding up his burly but probably unruly teammates to help, he commissioned his five-foot, size-two girlfriend. I suspect that he made this choice both to avoid flak from time away from her and to bring some pleasure to the task. Together they pulled up the sod between the bases and raked the outfield to life. It was hard, heavy work, but perfectly suited for young adult bodies buzzing with spring fever. Clearing the sod took almost a month's time but progress was visible. The neighborhood started to notice. In time, the "rake and shovel" work was exhausted. To complete the project, Chris needed more specialized equipment to landscape the field back into a diamond. A neighbor adjacent to the field pitched in a sledgehammer, a tamp, and a roller. Chris' dad provided the rototiller.

In contrast to avoiding me as he had when in the throes of indecision about his Capstone, Chris now initiated reports of his progress with an air of ownership, competence, and confidence. He also never neglected to remind me how much hard work was involved. His girlfriend never missed the opportunity to do the same.

Just when I thought he was on third and coming into home, Chris reluctantly told me that he did not think he would be able to finish. I assumed he meant readying the field.

"This weekend is supposed to be beautiful, can't you finish it then?" I said.

"No, it isn't the field, it's the dust," Chris clarified.

"The what?" I asked.

"You know, the stone dust for the baselines. It costs $96 and I don't have the money," he lamented. I suggested he speak to the principal, since the baseball field was within the school district, and the principal appreciated and respected Chris a great deal. The school donated half the money and his family the rest. When you don't have cash, use charm.

The stone dust was spread on the baselines and raked. "My final touch would be to place all the bases on the field and mow again the day before my presentation," Chris wrote in his fieldwork report.

The before-and-after pictures were breathtaking, and to actually visit the field was awe-inspiring. A real resurrection. The luscious spring-green field almost seemed out of place in contrast to the surrounding lawns, where the still-matted lifeless looking grass was yet to awake after being buried under ten feet of snow, ice, and freezing rain.

Chris' Capstone made the front page of the local newspaper in a lead article entitled "Field of Dreams: In the Field," alluding to both the baseball field and his goal of architectural engineering.[1] In the article staff writer Gary Hawkins pointed out that the project had unintended benefits. Not only did Chris revitalize a field but also potentially an arm of the neighborhood, the Community Club. There is hope that the need to maintain the field will revitalize the Community Club by bringing in new members to support the new generation of youth in the neighborhood.

In my book, Chris had hit a homer. He built his diamond by pulling up sod and laying down stone dust. He built and left a legacy.

In his Reflection Paper Chris wrote:

> By restoring this field I am overwhelmed by what I have done for the neighborhood children who have dreams of playing in the Majors themselves. It is quite the feeling to have kids all excited about baseball like I was when I chose this topic . . .. It gives me a sense of accomplishment and of what I will look forward to in my college and career days as an Architectural Engineer. In order to be

satisfied with your work, you must also satisfy others. I feel I have satisfied the kids in the neighborhood, and in the future they will keep baseball and this community field in their memories. It has been a pleasure.

Postscript: Chris earned a degree in architecture from Keene State College and now works for a sustainability company that builds new, "green" homes and retrofits old ones.

10

Senior Capstone

Release of the Beast

The auditorium was rocking. It was filled beyond capacity and was probably in violation of fire codes. Students were sitting in the aisles and standing in the back. Even after the doors closed, students outside the auditorium banged and begged for entrance. Scanning the packed auditorium, the principal asked, "Is there anyone in class?" Students gave up lunch and skipped their classes to see the much-anticipated unveiling of the original automosextacycle, a six-man cycle, affectionately dubbed *Green Thunda, The Beast*. Senior Capstone team Max and Joe—M&J—had plastered *Release the Beast* posters at entrances and exits, on bathrooms doors and lockers throughout the school. Their promotion worked. Classes were empty and the auditorium was bursting.

Team M&J had logged over 200 hours of work on the design and construction of the automosextacycle. *Green Thunda* deserved more than a mere presentation. Rather, to unveil their creation, M&J planned an extravaganza that would leave PowerPoint far behind.

Even after the students settled into their seats, they still fidgeted with anticipation. Finally, Max and Joe, professionally dressed, stepped out from behind the curtain, into the spotlight, and up to the podium. Struggling with nervous speech, they introduced their topic, covered their research on green energy, and projected a photo chronicle onto the big screen of the design and construction of the six-man cycle. The audience listened quietly, but tension was mounting. M&J quickly moved through the presentation requirements including expressions of gratitude and thanks to all those who had helped them with their Capstone. All bases were covered; nothing was left unsaid. They wasted no time by switching into high gear. The rest of the time was their own: Show Time!

M&J proceeded to strip off their dress shirts and pants to uncover their cycling uniform: *Green Thunda* sleeveless T-shirts and black athletic shorts. The principal, seated in front, looked around the auditorium asking, "Anyone filming this?" The curtains opened and the show began. The YouTube video, dubbed *Release of The Beast*, begins with a hysterical introduction of the six cyclists as they prepare for the inaugural ride.[1] In succession, each cyclist, dressed in the Green Thunda uniform, is shown either rising out of bed or coming out of a closet, bobbing his head to the beat of a La Bouche tune. After a short calisthenics warm-up to prepare for the ride of their lives, the six-man team line up at the closed garage door ready to face and tame *The Beast*. Slowly, the garage door lifts. *The Beast* awaits the boys as if daring them to break him in. Wheeling *The Beast* out of its "cage," the six-man team jumps on and rides away under a fresh spring canopy and onto the street.

After an arousing applause for the video, the audience quickly grew quiet. There was more to come. It was time to unveil the actual automosextacycle. The screen lifted; the stage was dark. The sound system played "Gonna Fly Now," the theme song from *Rocky*. To my astonishment, dry ice vapor billowed onto the stage from the wings. The principal shook his head and looked down. Dry ice is a no-no in school. The stage lights slowly turned up and there it was: *Green Thunda, The Beast,* slowly revolving on a huge makeshift turntable made by Team M&J especially for this occasion. The turntable was powered by one of the riders pulling a rope from behind the curtain. A roar went up, followed by lengthy applause and a standing ovation. The audience hesitantly shuffled out of their seats, hanging back, looking around for some cue. "Are they Capped?" a group of students yelled in unison. I answered affirmatively. The students ran to the main lobby to create the human arch for the Capping ceremony. The human arch for the M&J team was the largest yet, filling two whole hallways. Max and Joe rode *Green Thunda,* the automosextacycle, through the arch to their "Capping."

After the extravaganza was over, I debriefed Max and Joe in my classroom. They were visibly tired but the adrenaline was still pumping through their veins. "I was here until 11:00 last night and again this morning at 6:00, setting up the stage," said Max. I could see the shadows under his eyes. I smiled and leaned back in my chair with my arms dangling down toward the floor. I sighed, slowly releasing my own fatigue. I was tired, too. I had processed 90-plus Senior Capstones in one month's time, and there were still a few incompletes dangling out there like my arms. I looked across the table at Max and Joe and felt a swell of gratitude, not just for work well done but also for a new angle and a new attitude. Unexpectedly and almost without thought, out of my mouth came the words, "Thanks for making my year." They had showcased not only their own project with substance and pizzazz, but also the Capstone program itself.

The physics teacher at the high school called the automosextacycle "an engineering feat." But it was also intended to be a "going-green project." It synthesized Max and Joe's two special interests, engineering and fitness, respectively.

By 2008, M&J's senior year, "going green" was really catching on, especially among youth. "Going green" meant environmentally conscious living, using products specifically designed to reduce air pollution and conserve energy. Reducing your carbon footprint was in. Recycling, unplugging, quick showering, and zip-car driving had hit college campuses.

Team M&J had an innovative approach to recycling, beyond paper and plastic. They gave a new meaning to the word re-*cycle*. Instead of simply bicycling, try sextacyling (*sexta* meaning "six" in Latin). As Max wrote in his Capstone paper, "The average passenger car emits 115 pounds of smog-forming emissions each year. If one automosextacycle were used instead of a car, it would reduce smog-forming emissions by 690 pounds per year. It is a new way of carpooling and exercise, as well as a social event. Riding the automosextacycle is fun, safe, and healthy for the passengers and the environment."

The design of the cycle-for-six might have been more symbolic than practical in terms of "going green," but M&J's Capstone was a model in another sense. It demonstrated how to *do* a Capstone. M&J chose a project that ranked high in both interest and challenge for them. They chose a theme, "going green," that was topical and related to the greater world. M&J synthesized preexisting knowledge, both technical and life skills, as well as new skills learned specifically for this project. They brought a design drawn on paper to life. They recycled discarded bicycle parts and learned to weld. They worked effectively as a team and recruited six cyclists whom they would later recycle as a crew for Max's entrepreneurial painting business.

In his advice to future seniors, team leader Max suggested, "Try something that people say can't be done and do it. . . . You can do anything you put your mind to." He deliberately followed this up with a challenge: "Topping the automosextacycle can't be done." Of course, this is exactly what upcoming seniors tried to do. Raise the bar and they will rise to reach it.

In high school, a generation is four years. It takes at least four years to create change. Team M&J were in the fourth year of the Capstone program. They were the evidence of cultural change. It was no accident that their Capstone was seen by so many. The Senior Capstone was out of the wings; it had taken center stage. It was cool, dry ice and all. Shift happens. Deep sigh.

Postscript: In college, Max majors in mechanical engineering with a minor in business, and Joe majors in physical education. For summer employment, Max became a regional manager for *Collegiate Painting*, for which he won an award. He had his six-man crew, including his assistant manager, Joe, all lined up—recycled from his Capstone.

11

Senior Capstone

Out of Time

Andrew often ate lunch at the principal's table, where he had a listening audience. Conversation at the crowded student tables was a free-for-all with everyone talking and no one listening. Andrew loved to talk uninterrupted and could extinguish anyone who attempted to interject during his monologues on pet topics.

Andrew seemed to have a handle on himself despite the fact that he was missing part of his hands, a condition he was born with. He played his sport not on the field, but on the chessboard. He was a master chess player and could make moves that crushed his opponent early in the match.

He also knew a lot about wolves—their habitats, behavioral habits, social structure, and endangerment of extinction. It would not surprise me if Andrew had a wolf poster hanging on the back of his bedroom door.

"The wolf got a bad rap from fairy tales and ranchers," said Andrew.

"Actually, wolves are really smart and social. They're not dangerous unless protecting their young or territory." But misperceptions die hard.

When it came time to select his Capstone, a teacher who knew Andrew well suggested wolves for his topic. After all, Andrew's knowledge base and strong interest in wolves would make for a good head start on the Capstone.

Andrew acquiesced to what initially seemed like an easy way out. I sensed his thinking: *What the heck. I might as well just do my Capstone on wolves and get it over with.*

Weeks went by and he had not done any work on his tentative wolf Capstone. No proposal, no research, no mentor, no plan for fieldwork. The project was dead on the desk.

Some faculty suggested that the Capstone was beyond him; it had too many parts and was too complex. It overwhelmed him; that is why he had shut down. I thought otherwise, especially after sitting with him at the principal's table for lunch on several occasions.

When one too many weeks went by, I called Andrew in for a conference. "Andrew, do you really want to do your Capstone on wolves?"

Avoiding eye contact and the truth, he shrugged, saying, "Yeah, it's okay."

"'Okay?!'" I exclaimed. In my head I was shouting, *That word! Blah. Noncommittal. Complacent. Compromising.*

Softening my tone, I exhaled, "*Okay* is not going to get you there."

"I still have time," he answered, not yet wanting to leave the safety of wolves.

"No, you don't! You do not have time to spend on a project that you do not want to do," I retorted. "The worst thing that you can do is waste your time on a topic that you are done with and outgrown; it bores you. The problem here is *boredom*. Your time and life are far too valuable to just jump through a hoop."

Silence. He pondered, looking out the window at the athletic fields and woods beyond.

I waited and let his mind wander. When his attention came back into the room, I gently asked, "Andrew, what are you curious about? What fascinates you?"

He paused, grimaced as if trying to fit a vast idea into the confines of the classroom. I waited. He looked down at his desk and shook his head.

"What is it?" I inquired.

"No, it could never be," he said in resignation.

"What?" I asked more insistently.

"Well . . .," he hesitated.

"Try me," I chided with hands on hips.

"I don't know . . . you'll think I'm weird . . . it's kind of out there."

"Well, that makes two of us." I said.

"Well, okay then . . . time travel. I want to know if it is possible."

"You're on," I retorted and exited the room with a straight face.

After my exit, I caught my breath in the hallway. *Yikes! What did I just do? Sign on to time travel? Am I out of my mind?* Where does time travel belong—science fiction or science fact? Or did it belong somewhere in between? Would this topic hold up as a legitimate Capstone? What in the world would Andrew do for fieldwork? My mind was whirling and needed grounding.

In my panic, I sought out Mr. Conway, the senior science teacher, directly after school. Andrew was in Mr. Conway's homeroom, so the two had a preexisting bond. Not unlike Andrew, I too was reluctant to spit out the topic in question to Mr. Conway. Surprisingly, Conway was not at all daunted by the idea of time travel. In relief, I exhaled deeply. Scratching his head, Mr. Conway attempted to reassure me. "I'll make a couple of contacts and get back to you," he said.

In less than a week Conway had networked his way to Ronald Mallet, an eminent theoretical physicist at the University of Connecticut known for his work on time travel and author of the popular book, *Time Traveler.*[1] Conway handed me Mallet's phone number and e-mail address, saying, "Good luck." I took it from there.

Dr. Mallet responded immediately. We spoke on the phone and he agreed to work with Andrew. The two exchanged e-mails multiple times, with Dr. Mallet feeding Andrew material on time travel and its related physics.

The topic of time travel was amply legitimized when Dr. Mallet gave a lecture and demonstration on the physics of time travel from UConn via closed circuit TV to a standing-room-only class bulging with physical science students.

It was the possibility of time travel that fascinated Dr. Mallet as a boy and was the impetus for pursuing the study of physics as a man. His beloved father had died of a heart attack when Ronald was ten years old. As a young boy missing his father, Dr. Mallet dreamed of going back in time to prevent his loss. Certainly there are misfortunes and tragic events in many lives that we would prevent if it were at all possible. Perhaps it was this desire that brought Dr. Mallet and Andrew together.

With the assistance of Mr. Conway, Andrew made a miniature model of Dr. Mallet's time machine, a configuration of lasers and mirrors. It was evident from Andrew's Capstone paper and presentation that he understood the applicable theories of physics, a synthesis of Einstein's work on relativity and space-time, as well as Dr. Mallet's work on circulating laser light relative to time travel. Remarkable. The idea is to bend time back on itself through the swirling of space.

An aspect of time travel that most intrigues students is the grandmother paradox. Meaning, what happens if you time travel and accidentally kill your grandmother so she could never give birth to your father?

What if Andrew did not dare share what truly interested him for his Capstone? The science students and faculty within the high school would never be introduced to the possibility of time travel from a physics perspective. Andrew might never realize his proclivity for theoretical science closing the gap between imagination and reality. His question about the possibility of time travel would have gone unanswered.

Andrew wrote in his Capstone reflection paper, "It was intellectually challenging for me because I was on second and the ball was heading for the Andromeda Galaxy. . . . I knew almost nothing about time travel before this. . . . I answered my essential question. . . . I feel wonderful. . . . I did something that not many could do and understand. I grew personally from the Capstone experience because I learned that I don't have to have the answers and I don't have to be perfect. My greatest strength was my ability to think outside the box."

12

Senior Capstone

Bandana Man

Bandana Man—not a nickname, but a signature accessory. Zack had a collection of bandanas that kept his shoulder-length golden hair from falling into his face of gentle strength. *Collected*, is how I would describe him. Private and steady, a watcher, a "senser," a thinker. It seemed he was often occupied in the amorphous sea of Mind, listening to free-floating sounds and rhythms on the surface that would lead him into the deep beyond.

Zack had been mulling over the idea of a rock opera for some time—years, I suspect. He used the Capstone as his chance and reason to write one. Quite deliberately, he embarked on his rock opera, *Raven*, on the first day of the New Year, the year of his graduation, the year he would step into adulthood.

I never bothered Zack during Capstone lab. The one or two times I did call on him, it was not to check if he was "present," but to be sure he was not. I could feel that he was in a creative mode behind that bandana of his. He was deep in the zone. He didn't want to talk about his rock opera, not because of a lack of progress, but because of the risk. If he talked about it, the drive to write it would dissipate and be gone. It would already be expressed. I wondered if his bandana was a kind of shield to keep creative powers in and intrusions out.

One possibility for a Senior Capstone is to take a skill to another level or in another direction. That is the course that Zack chose. He was an accomplished guitarist and singer, had studied music theory, and experimented with composition. To write his rock opera, Zack had to synthesize and stretch his talent, knowledge, and skills to the max. Before *Raven* was finished, Zack would compose and arrange music; write lyrics; direct, record, and produce the opera onto a CD.

Rock operas intrigued Zack. His favorites were *Tommy* and *Jesus Christ Superstar*. It was storytelling through music. The blend of rock and opera might seem unnatural at first, but they have common roots. As Zack wrote in his Capstone paper, "Rock, having its roots deep in the blues, is a form of music that relies heavily on storytelling. Songs are generally steeped in personal emotion. Opera is a genre which is all about storytelling. . . . The different musical styles and stigmas of the genres fall away and they become two of the closest linked varieties of music imaginable."

Raven was a total of 17 original songs that took at least 200 hours to compose over a period of almost five months. Zack's parents reported that he was up late at night and into early morning hours working on *Raven*. They marveled at his self-motivation. While Zack had always been on top of his studies, his parents had never witnessed this degree of ownership and drive. He seemed obsessed.

Creating is like that. It is akin to "compulsing." There is no choice. Once a creation catches fire by the breath of its creator, it takes on a life of its own; it won't leave you alone. It takes up occupancy in the mind and pesters until it is released. Rather than you writing it, it turns and starts to write you, or at least through you. It comes when you leave the mundane world and enter the dream where creating happens. Bob Dylan, a living icon, writer of timeless lyrics, and recipient of an honorary doctorate in poetry from Princeton, once explained that his lyrics were just *there* and if he didn't write them down, someone else would. I suspect that, at school, Zack was in the dream state as much as he could afford it and then went home and transcribed in the privacy of his room, uninterrupted, late into the night.

Coincidentally, Zack's rock opera, *Raven*, was set in a dream. I wonder if that made it safe for Zack. After all, it was just a dream.

It is not easy to unveil a complete work of art, to be vulnerable and expose the inner self. The reality of his dream to compose a rock opera was no more evident than when he handed out a booklet of all seventeen songs to members of his audience at the beginning of his Capstone presentation. He skillfully related what he'd learned about the roots and architecture of rock opera, and then shared his process in writing and composing *Raven*, playing samples of the songs as he described the story line.

Raven is an archetypal tale of good versus evil. The focus is on a "baseless" band of hapless musicians that was going nowhere. "Their tone is awful, their rhythms are off, their lyrics uninspired at best. . . ." Members of the band are unable to appreciate anything in the "wrapped, packaged, and stale world." The band has a chance to get back on track with their music and life when they meet Raven, a wise man posing as a street musician, who creates "unbelievable music." In indigenous cultures, the raven bird is believed to expose the truth and symbolizes transformation and change.

Raven, the wise man, focuses his efforts on Will, the main character, who has fallen in with Evil. Will wants life to be easy and is "taste-testing" Evil; he does not want to think for himself or take responsibility for his life. He wants someone else to give him the answers. Raven tells Will not to be afraid of the "Beyond," but to leave safe havens of convenience and be a leader for the good.

Friends plead with Will to listen to Raven's wisdom:

> Oh, Listen, Listen. . . . He said Love, Love is what is right. . . .
> And you all said, Yeah, we know all about love,
> And you went right on doing all the hurting, all the hating, all the hard luck brother-ing that you always done before. . . .
> And you'll all of you do it again,
> Unless you listen to someone who really loves,
> And you know, yes you know, you know he does. . . .[1]

During this final song of Zack's rock opera, there was a reverent, almost sacred silence in the darkened auditorium. No one spoke, but there was a response. Tears. And I was not the only one. What moved us so? Was it the message of the law of life being love, or was it the scope and scale of Zack's creative achievement? Was it witnessing the fruition of a dream for someone so young? All together, it was almost overwhelming. Long, slow breath. More silence. Rather than praise, words of gratitude were the first to come. "Thank you, Zack." "Beautiful." "Inspiring."

There were no more than ten people in attendance at Zack's Capstone presentation. Zack had wanted it that way. This was not for a big school assembly. Nor would Zack give a school performance of *Raven* when he was asked. He was done. It was finished.

As we rose from our seats to leave, I reached out to Zack's parents. They were awestruck. This was the first time they had heard any of their son's rock opera. Zack's mother said, "I had no idea this was in him. I did not know that he understood [the law of life]. I don't know if I ever would have if he had not done this. I am amazed that someone so young understands." I was not sure Zack would have, either, if he had not done his rock opera. It led him into the beyond—and he listened.

I looked back to the stage where Zack was gathering up his sound equipment. It was then that I saw him take off his bandana. It had done its job.

Postscript: Zack studies contemporary classical composition and classical, jazz, and flamenco guitar in college.

13

Senior Capstone

Saturated by Silence

"American culture is sex saturated but sex silent," was the opening statement of Matt's Capstone presentation and paper entitled *Sex Education, A Cross-Cultural Perspective.* He continued:

> Sex is all over television, movies, and music, but we lack meaningful education and serious discussion of the issue. There is a common belief that withholding information and services will lead to responsible sexual behavior. Yet the opposite appears to be true. . . . In America we tell teens to "just say no" and leave young people in the dark with little access to services or guidance. This proves to be an egregious error.

Matt had a chiseled voice that did not waste words. He was thoughtful in his speech as if he mulled over what he was going to say before he opened his mouth. When he did speak, he always said something worth listening to. He had a commanding presence behind the lectern. Matt was tall, fit, and tan— the picture of health and vitality. He tended to squint his eyes when he smiled.

When talking about sex education, he did not squint, but scowled. He felt the existing curriculum was slanted towards the hazards of sex, rather than its positive and healthy aspects. Matt felt that society was promoting abstinence as a solution to sexual issues amongst youth. The core of sex education focused on risks: pregnancy, STDs, HIV, and date rape. Certainly, these are real problems and students should be educated on the risks. But Matt wanted to learn about the social and emotional meaning of such a powerful human experience as sexuality. Matt was in search of a broader perspective for sex education.

Matt was not interested in studying human sexuality as a Capstone topic. It was too wide a sweep. The focus needed to be narrowed down and put in the context of his concern about sex education in high school.

Matt also had his eye on his Capstone presentation. He did not want to *teach* about human sexuality. He wanted to make an impact and be a catalyst for change in the high school's sex education curriculum—and to make a difference for students who followed. He was on a mission, a man of action. But to get the job done, he needed a more comprehensive model for sex education.

Matt felt caught between two worlds: the promotion of abstinence, on one hand, and the current culture of casual sex and "hooking up," on the other. Neither seemed particularly appealing.

Finding a suitable mentor was a challenge. I sought the help of David, the school social worker, my colleague and friend. "Do you know a psychologist or social worker who might be a mentor on the topic of sex education?" I asked. No one came to David's mind. After some discussion, we both agreed that the most appropriate mentor would be an educator. A couple of days later, David got back to me quite excited about his find. "My daughter took a course on human sexuality at the university and was wild about the professor. She said there is always a waiting list to get into the course." I crossed my fingers.

Surprisingly, given the demands on her time and attention, Professor Sandy Caron of the University of Maine was responsive and willing to be a mentor for Matt. Dr. Caron quickly picked up on Matt's earnestness, his genuine interest, and his call for change. The knowledge that Dr. Caron shared with Matt was exactly what he was seeking. Dr. Caron had done original research and had written several books focusing on cross-cultural models of sex education that were comprehensive and addressed psychosocial and emotional issues. She shared with Matt a vast number of academic sources on models for comprehensive sex education.

Finally Matt had a mentor, a legitimate authority in the study of human sexuality, to help guide and direct his Capstone. But most important, Matt now had support for his perspective and views on sex education.

Together, Matt and his Dr. Caron developed a survey for his fieldwork. The anonymous and optional survey was given only to seniors under the controlled conditions of the Senior Capstone labs. Seventy percent of the senior class took the survey. Gender was almost evenly divided: 52 percent female, 48 percent male. The survey was divided into two parts. The first section focused on sex education: sources of information and range of topics covered. The one open-ended question asked: "What do you wish you were taught about sex in school or from your parents?" The second section queried beliefs about sex, asking for degrees of agreement with statements such as "I can be popular without having sex," and "I am sure I can discuss my beliefs about sex with my parent."

Dr. Caron had encouraged Matt to include a behavioral section in the survey, but Matt did not think that he would get valid results or administrative approval.

Not surprisingly, students ranked friends as their number-one source of information about sex, whereas parents were last.

In ranking topics in order of importance, safe sex, birth control, and where to obtain birth control were at the top. Abstinence was at the bottom. Students' responses to what they wanted to be taught by school or parents included: what sex is, the importance of sex, how to have sex and how to please your significant other. Several comments conveyed the feeling that sex "is not a bad thing to want." One student wanted "less about the 'devilishness' of it and more about not letting it define you." Beliefs about sex: 96 percent of females, and 88 percent of males believe they can be popular without having sex; 61 percent of females and 40 percent of males believe it is acceptable to have sex only after a relationship becomes serious; 96 percent of both males and females are sure they would *always* use some form of birth control.

Matt summarized what he learned from Dr. Caron by contrasting the United States with Northern European countries with respect to teen sex:

> The United States has the highest rates of teen pregnancies, abortions, births, and STDs compared to other industrialized countries such as the United Kingdom, Sweden, Canada, and France. Youth in these countries become sexually active around the same age (16–17) as Americans. In comparison to these other countries, U.S. teens are more likely to have more partners, less meaningful relationships, and are more inclined to experiment.

Matt highlighted the fact that sex education is commonplace and well integrated into the school curriculum in Northern European countries. Contraception is cheap, easily accessible, and seemingly effective in the prevention of teen pregnancy. Matt emphasized that not only do students in Northern European countries learn about the physical and health aspects of sex but also the relational, emotional and psychological aspects. "Sexual fidelity rather than abstinence is encouraged. The deeper meaning and experience that can be found in sex is worth seeking," explained Matt.

Matt argued that sex education does not open the door to promiscuity, but quite the opposite:

> It is clear that sex education in schools is lacking and so is sex education at home. Students are interested in learning more. Leaving it up to friends seems to be leaving it up to chance. Research has shown that education and access to services are key to helping young people develop healthy sexual relationships. [Sex education] does not encourage earlier sexual behavior. It does not increase sexual activity. What it does is encourage young people to take responsibility.

Matt referenced an article entitled: "Good Sex: Why We Need More of It and a Lot Less of the Bad Stuff," by Jennifer Roback Morse, research fellow at Stanford's Hoover Institution. Morse's article supports Matt's plea for learning about the positive side of sex. Morse writes, "I have found through my own experience that it's extremely difficult to figure out the meaning of human sexuality on your own. . . By the time you have conducted enough trials and errors to learn that your initial premises were false, you've lost a lot of time. . . This is part of what older people ought to offer younger people: the benefit of experience and hindsight. That way you don't have to make it all up as you go along."[1] Exactly.

The analysis and presentation of Matt's research and survey results coupled with his argument for a more positive, social and emotional approach to sex education caught the attention of the principal. Changes were made in the sex-education curriculum that addressed some of Matt's concerns. Matt had achieved his Capstone goal of being a catalyst for change in the sex education curriculum. That was reason enough to replace Matt's scowl with a smile.

Postscript: Matt graduated from the University of Maine with a double major in anthropology and history.

14

Senior Capstone

Going Afield

First and foremost—fieldwork. Fieldwork is the seniors' favorite part of the Capstone. Seniors stretched themselves to experience life above the North Pole, to take underwater photos in the Atlantic, and to build a desk from multiples woods harvested from Grandpa's 1,000 acres.

Fieldwork is always tricky business. There is much to consider. First of all, is it legal? Does it meet the approval of parents and the school administration? Will it engender new learning? Is there an ample challenge and learning stretch? Is it worthy of the senior? Is there a high level of interest (a rating 9 or 10 on a 1–10 scale), sustainable over six or more months? No reruns of old work, hoop jumps just to get it done, or piggybacking on others' work allowed. The Capstone, by its very nature, needs to be fresh, new.

Laura and Kate took all these considerations to heart in choosing their fieldwork. These two creatures accustomed to comfort wanted to go *afield* for their fieldwork—far afield into the wilderness, away from it all. Both Laura and Kate had been raised with great care and oversight, not exactly sheltered but closely tended. I was a bit wary of their idea. *Wilderness? These two?* It did not seem to fit. It crossed my mind they might be taking "getting outside your comfort zone" a bit too far.

I knew that both Laura and Kate could rise to big challenges; both were high-achieving students. They were both positive in attitude and presentation. Laura was a star athlete. Kate was a leader in student government and an active member of both Academic Decathlon and Amnesty International.

Laura and Kate were not above giggling when talking about their "wild" Capstone idea. They loved to imagine survival in the rawness of the wilderness. Killing and skinning a squirrel or rabbit for food. "Ha, ha." Encounters with black bear and moose. "Ohhh my." A sudden cloudburst soaking them through. "Brrr . . ." Digging a poop hole. "Yuck!" Coyotes and wolves howling in the distance. And don't forget the legendary mountain lions in the wilds of Maine. What about poachers? Which is more dangerous, man or beast? "We're going to need a gun or a knife that could do some serious damage," they joked. More laughter.

Neither Laura nor Kate had any camping experience, let alone wilderness experience. Each came from a family of two girls, no boys. Backpacking in the Grand Canyon or whitewater rafting on the Colorado River was not on the family to-do list. Rather, it was sandy beaches in the Caribbean on spring break.

More than one pair of guys in their class commented, "Hey, we're thinking of doing that for *our* Capstone. I bet you two back out." This made Laura and Kate laugh some more and made them even wilder about their Capstone. Landing a wilderness Capstone ahead of the boys was satisfying in itself.

Laura and Kate were equally cavalier about their mothers' concerns and reservations that they brushed aside with untested confidence. Their fathers seemed more open and sought to help. Understandably, the parents' concerns were about safety and their daughters' total lack of experience in the wild. Where could they go? Camping in public parks would provide neither a wilderness experience nor much of a challenge. Where the wilderness held the threat of beast, public parks held the threat of man.

Ironically, a Maine Guide, who was recommended as a mentor by a friend of Laura's father, had been indicted for sexual misconduct while working at a summer camp— unbeknownst, of course, to Laura's father or his friend. It was Kate's mother who coincidentally found out about the indictment when casually mentioning her daughter's Capstone to a co-worker. This revelation almost folded the wilderness Capstone.

The silliness was gone. Having their Capstone threatened, Laura and Kate became serious and got to work, real work. They sought out mentors through scouting and the Outing Club at Colby College. Kate and Laura each chose research topics that related to their purpose in seeking a wilderness experience: ecopsychology and detaching from the materialism of society, respectively.

After an all-out search by both families for a suitable and safe location for a wilderness experience, a place was finally found—a 90-acre property in Northern Maine that belonged to a friend of Kate's father. Interestingly, this family friend was building a self-sustaining home off the grid of land he had bonded with as a boy. Finally, the girls had a green light for their Capstone.

"The land we stayed on was completely secluded and let us feel like we were in bona fide wilderness, while still having the safety of a person to go to with [any] problems," wrote Laura. "The location was key since we wanted to be completely separated from society and other people."

One damp evening after a steady day of rain, I lounged on the couch at home and skimmed through both Laura's and Kate's Capstone papers. Resting the papers on my chest, I closed my eyes and soaked in the contents. I breathed deep with appreciation from what I had just read. Through their respective research, Laura and Kate had unearthed truths and clarified the meaning and purpose of their wilderness experience. It was not a test of survival. Rather, it was to totally separate from society in order to deepen their connection to and their bond with nature and each another.

Kate's truth: Humans not only come from nature, but *are* nature. When we lose that connection, we lose a part of our own nature and we suffer accordingly. Ecopsychology uses psychology to understand the connection between humanity and the earth, how a weak connection can be harmful to both earth and the human soul, and how a reestablished connection can heal both.

Laura's truth: The focus on consumption at the expense of connection has undermined relationships, health, and well-being, both individually and collectively. The illusion of wealth as a means to well-being just does not hold up, whereas strong interpersonal ties and care of the community do.

Still, these "knowings" written in their Capstone papers were of the mind but not yet wholly experienced in the heart, body, and soul. It was one thing to know it and yet another to live it. Only by living it does one own it.

Once in the wild, Laura and Kate wanted to use only the resources they could find and gather. Their shelter was made with evergreen branches and boughs. They cooked over a fire made from hard-to-find dry kindling and burnable wood scavenged from the damp early-spring forest floor.

After their return from the wilderness, Kate wrote:

> Through my research, I learned and understood the concepts of having a connection with nature, but through my fieldwork, I was able to experience it, bringing an entire[ly] new dimension to my learning. . . . This type of out-of-the-classroom learning is vital in achieving a fulfilling education.

As for Laura, she wrote,

> Learning outside the classroom is a key component
> to anyone's education. Secondary information is
> important, but ultimately one-sided. When one is
> able to experience something for themselves, that
> person is much more likely to hold that knowledge
> in high regard.
>
> Sleeping on the ground, bad hygiene, and
> constant swarms of black flies does not exactly
> sound relaxing; however, I returned home more
> refreshed and stress-free than after a long weekend
> at home. Society does take a toll on [a] person, and
> I believe our fieldwork demonstrates the
> importance of human and nature interaction.

The stillness of the wild was almost palatable in Laura
and Kate' video shown at their Capstone presentation. The only
sounds were solitary: the crackling fire, the shuffling of rain
pants, the clanging of camp cookware. The only view was the
dense mixed forest that held the soft tones of their few but
deliberate words. Perhaps it was the clarity of the air that
carried the sounds so cleanly.

That is what one first notices when going to the North
Woods of Maine. The air is so clear that it enlivens the whole
body with each breath. Any man-made noise heard from afar
are muffled by the mountains. Thoughts slow down. The heart
beats slower but stronger. You are a guest in the North Woods.
You are humbled. The wild rules. These senses came through
even in the brief ten-minute video, which attested to the
authenticity of Laura and Kate's fieldwork. Their presentation
was over all too soon. I wanted to skip my next class and stay
in the wild.

Laura and Kate had done the unexpected with their
inexperience. They surpassed mere survival and succeeded in
connecting to and bonding with nature and each another. They
lay skin to skin with the earth. They covered and sheltered

themselves with her branches. They discovered that fire shielded them from the merciless biting of black flies, which almost drove them out. The wild satiated their senses, releasing them from the need for distraction. Boredom never entered camp.

During their presentation, Laura and Kate discussed their heightened sense of independence and self-reliance from their wilderness experience. But perhaps the greatest and most applicable growth was their ability to solve problems and overcome the roadblocks that had threatened their Capstone. It was these barriers that tested their resolve and strengthened both their commitment and their determination to follow through. Instead of learning to kill and skin a squirrel for survival, they learned to navigate through the quagmire of their own "wild" Capstone.

Postscript: Laura attends Bowdoin College and Kate attends Wheaton College. Both major in sociology.

15

Senior Capstone

Portrait of School, Portrait of Self

Alexa, the valedictorian of her class, had earned the right to challenge the educational system. After all, she had done everything asked of her as a student, to the point of perfection. She strove without pause and at times even sacrificed her health. She was at the top of her class.

After studying abroad in Argentina during her junior year, Alexa returned home a changed student. She dared to skip school for the first time. She challenged her teachers. "Why are we doing this assignment?" "What is the purpose of it?" "Why is it important?" For the first time, Alexa was late with homework assignments, and sometimes she did not do them at all. She came and went from school according to her own needs and whims. She started hanging out with friends more and widened her social circle.

It was in a different hemisphere, continent, and time zone that she turned off the automatic and learned to shift gears. This gave her more speed options by which to live her life. For Alexa, the year abroad was not only an immersion in a foreign language and culture but also in a lifestyle that was a world apart. The pace was very different in Argentina. To get around, Alexa walked, biked, or ran. Every mid-afternoon she gathered together with her Argentinean friends for *mate*.

The reentry into high school back home was not a comfortable one. At first there was the indignity of hall passes and arguments about senior privileges with the administration. The required classes that she had missed while in Argentina did not challenge or engage her. Alexa deemed lengthy homework assignments as busywork and intolerable. Alexa was revved up—torn between the lifestyle she lived while in Argentina that was more balanced and healthy, and the high-stress American lifestyle that was the road to "success."

When it came time to choose her Capstone topic, Alexa, like most seniors, focused first on what to *do* for fieldwork. Alexa wanted to paint, to expand beyond paper/pencil drawings. Her "signature" pieces were pencil-drawn portraits that delighted her friends at home and abroad. For her Capstone, though, she did an about-face and chose to paint a self-portrait in color on canvas. However, Alexa had no interest in researching self-portraits beyond learning that it was an important phase in an artist's development. "How about researching an area of educational reform?" I asked. "That seems to be an area that you are all about these days."

"But about what?" she asked. For Alexa, the problem was not a matter of curriculum, instructional methods, or programs. It was the whole system. "No one dares question an institution so deeply entrenched in society," Alexa stated. "No one dares to redefine learning, but I do."

What had been a vague discontentment with school before Argentina became much clearer to Alexa upon her return. "Every day I get up in the morning and go through the motions that society calls 'education.' Every night I slave away at homework to score high on a test and then forget what I 'learned.'"

Alexa was excited about her inaugural self-portrait but less certain about her research. "What does educational reform have to do with painting a self-portrait? How do they connect?" she asked.

"They must, somehow, because they both came from and are important to you," I answered. At that time I truly did not know the connection but felt it would emerge during the process of doing her Capstone. I opted for student choices in research and fieldwork that held high levels of interest in both, even if, at first, the research and fieldwork were seemingly unrelated. So it was decided—school reform and self-portrait. The connection was there but Alexa needed to *do* her fieldwork first.

Alexa entitled her research paper, the *Dissociation of School and Learning.* That was her realization as she stood at the top, looking down at the endless hours of homework, study, tests, anxiety about GPA and class rank, and deprivation of sleep and social life. Had her love of learning been wrung out of her as she ground out her homework?

Alexa read the works of educational reformers. She studied the history of public school education and its tie to the Industrial Age. She researched the perennial controversies about homework, grading, and ranking, and the more recent understandings of adolescent brain development. Through research, Alexa became acquainted with prominent visionaries who reflected her views. This gave her the footing and confidence to espouse a model of learning that was wholistic, self-directed, and community-based.

Now it was time to experience what she espoused. When "faced" with doing the Capstone, Alexa spoke honestly about the anxiety it aroused in her. "This project is a huge learning stretch for me. I rarely take complete control over my education. There is no right answer to my topic; and to follow my own structure will be difficult. I have never structured my own project or made connections between my written work and active [applied] research. The project topic is a risk . . . . The Capstone stretches my learning to about a nine on a one-to-ten scale."

Conversely, Alexa had played the school game and played it well. As she said in her Capstone paper, "the 'best students' know how to play to the judge." Years later, another valedictorian told me that those in the top ten of his graduating class were not necessarily the best and the brightest, rather they knew how to exploit teachers. System beaters. The game of school was about getting good grades rather than taking risks for the sake of learning.

Alexa was not alone in feeling that the challenge of self-directed learning and creating a Capstone was outside of her comfort zone and conditioning. It was a struggle. Customarily the teacher is in the driver's seat rather than the student. But some struggle is inherent in creating. Struggle should not be a sign to stop. Even Alexa's mentor, portrait painter Bonnie Spiegel, spoke of struggle as not something to be avoided, nor even something painful. "Enjoy the process [of painting the self-portrait]. Even the struggles are good. Above all, remember to have fun."

Alexa came to embrace the idea that the Capstone was an opportunity to learn and *do* what seniors always wanted to do but never had the excuse, permission or chance to do. Up until the Capstone, Alexa had limited her drawings to black and white. Alexa had never painted with color or on a canvas. Her self-portrait would be a first.

For inspiration and ideas, Alexa attended the opening of her mentor's portrait exhibition, entitled *Face to Face,* at a coastal gallery. What was most striking, almost shocking, in Spiegel's portraits was her use of brilliant color-every color! Spiegel used a full array of color in her painting of faces. No color was spared. It was as if to say that people are full of color and it was her goal to capture that on canvas.

Alexa took this in and experimented with color for her self-portrait. Using shades of green accentuated the somewhat impish expression on her face, with the eyes looking down and off to one side and lips somewhat pursed.

"It's a pleasure to see what you've accomplished," said Bonnie Spiegel in her final feedback on Alexa's self-portrait. "I especially like the gesture of your head. The animation you captured with that slight tilt and close viewpoint gave me a clue to your personality. And you seem to have captured a good likeness with an equally good grasp of your anatomy. I can tell you did a lot of hard looking. One of the interesting things about doing portraits is keeping a visual record of how you morph from moment to moment. There are so many sides to each of us to be explored, and documented. Keep painting!"

There was the connection. Alexa had morphed herself from the perfect student, the valedictorian of her class, into a successful self-directed learner—at least this one time. Learning was not all black and white, with right and wrong answers. Learning was full of color and of many shades. In her full-color self-portrait, Alexa had captured the self that was impish and a bit mischievous, someone who dared to challenge the status quo. She had earned the right.

Upon graduating, Alexa vowed that she would live a more balanced lifestyle in college. By both personal and second-hand accounts, that is exactly what she did without the sacrifice of her own success.

Postscript: Alexa graduated from Clark University with a major in Communication and Culture and minor in Innovation and Entrepreneurship. During college she co-founded a thrift store on campus. She holds a Master's degree in Professional Communications.

16

Senior Capstone

A Serious Business

Carl brought the house down with the story about what the Prom Committee aptly substituted for balloons when the supply ran short while decorating for the dance. "It was dark, so we didn't think anyone would notice." This opening warmed up the packed audience for Carl's Stand-Up-Comedy-Night that was the culmination of his Capstone on humor.

Then there was the joke about all the colored paper in the school copier. "I want to know who is responsible for all that colored paper in the paper trays of the school copiers!" Carl shouted. "Is this some kind of joke, reverse prank, or payback to seniors just before we graduate? Now this 'colors in the copier' routine has just gone too far and has got to stop!" Carl yelled. "There is not a copier anywhere in this school with regular white paper, not upstairs or down. What is worse is that there is not even enough of any one color to print off a multipage report; it starts off in forest green and ends up rosy red." How is a teacher supposed to take you seriously when you hand in an assignment dressed in baby pink and blue?" Carl sounded exasperated.

Carl was the slapstick comedian of the student body. He was easy to locate by his booming voice, which always sounded slightly hoarse from overdrive. Carl had an equally resounding presence and was an extrovert extraordinaire. He fed off attention in the classroom, or better yet, in front of a crowd. His forte' was in the stands at basketball games, charging up the fans as a one-man cheerleading squad, following his b-ball classmates to a victorious state championship. The night of the big game he filled the stands with fans dressed and/or painted in school colors. Banners were unfurled and horns blared. Carl knew how to compete in the stands and he made sure that his team of cheering fans did as well as the team on the court. The cheering squad that Carl "coached" over the course of the basketball season was certainly a factor in bringing home the golden ball.

Come Senior Capstone time, Carl questioned what more he could possibly do for the school. At least, that is how he saw it: "I am so involved; I'm on every committee—Yearbook (Editor), Homecoming, Prom, Senior Night. I practically run the place around here." In addition, Carl had been selected for Boys' State and was an active participant in Drama Club.

He did not know what else he had in him. Not surprisingly, he selected humor as his Capstone topic. "But what will I do with that?" Carl wondered. "Write jokes?"

His hero was stand-up comedian Bob Marley, dubbed Maine's King of Comedy. Efforts to contact Marley as a mentor went unanswered.

The principal knew of a local comedian who worked in the state department of education and moonlighted with a stand-up comedy act for large gatherings: reunions, special occasions, and meetings. He agreed to work with Carl and coached him on the elements of comedy: knowing and connecting with your audience, *delivering* rather than just *telling* a joke, practicing, and—above all—timing. Perhaps more importantly, he taught Carl that humor is serious business and can have a profound effect on health and healing. He shared with Carl the work of Norman Cousins, renowned author of *Anatomy of an Illness*, in which Cousins tells how humor helped him recover from a life-threatening illness.[1] "There is an element of truth in the old adage that laughter is the best medicine," explained Carl's mentor, who said that members of his audiences claimed to get relief from pain during his comedy acts.

Carl took his off-the-cuff, on-the-fly, hit-and-run humor to the next level when he held his audience in the palm of his hand for a night of comedy. He was hilarious. I can still remember howling in laughter and getting an endorphin high that lasted throughout the next day.

Carl not only delivered on his stand-up comedy but also used his captive audience to help Grace, a classmate in crisis who had lost all her personal belongings and irreplaceable memorabilia just days before in a fire that destroyed the home she shared with her grandmother and guardian.

News of the fire quickly spread and the school community was eager to help—maybe a bit too eager. Grace was highly sensitive, reserved, and private; she did not like all the attention that suddenly descended upon her, especially when she was struggling to cope with such a devastating loss. She let it be known through a faculty channel that she did not want handouts or money offered to her during school; she found it unnerving and embarrassing. Even though she was without the most basic necessities, she felt obliged to pay the money back but had no idea how she could ever do so.

Carl had a plan. Knowing that Grace would not be attending his Stand-Up Comedy Night, he saw it as chance to fundraise for Grace in a way that respected her dignity. In a most humble and sincere manner, Carl told the audience before the show that a donation box was being passed around for his classmate Grace; any donations would be greatly appreciated. The audience was generous and afterwards Grace was able to accept this support, since it was anonymous. Carl had melded two of his strengths, humor and a strong ethic of service, to help out his classmate in crisis.

Carl's first job out of college was giving tours at the Ben and Jerry's factory in Vermont. I think it is no accident that he works for a company that combines the pleasures of ice cream with a strong activism to improve the world. A colleague told me that he heard Ben and Jerry give an inspirational speech at a professional conference. In telling their story, Ben and Jerry attributed their rise from a small corner store in Burlington, Vermont, where they sold their homemade ice cream, to an internationally known ice cream brand by the fact that they always gave back, even when they were operating on a shoestring. Ben and Jerry supported activism for the environment, world peace, and social justice.

Carl, too, wanted to give back. In his reflection paper, he wrote:

> Something that was so cool and made me so proud was that we were able to raise money for the Rice family. I knew I was never going to be able to raise, by myself, the amount of money that I wanted to give her, but collectively my dream was more realistic.
>
> . . . Hearing people laugh and the responses I received because of my jokes gave me one of the best feelings I have ever felt. Words cannot describe how good I felt after that show, not because it was done, but because people enjoyed it.
>
> . . . We students take math, science, history, and English, and whether or not we take away something from the class is our choice. Senior Capstone almost forces you [to] take away something from the project. When you actually take something away from what you did, it allows

you to really reflect on it and use the really good things you learn and apply it to life.

...The Senior Capstone allowed me to be myself.

17

Senior Capstone

Second Hand

The auditorium was dark except for the stage, where a colorful montage of trendy clothing lighted up the screen. The audience was small and safe for Kim. Her parents were seated near the front, but off to one side. A handful of Kim's classmates huddled in the center. Everyone was quiet in anticipation. A few whispered softly. Not to intrude on the mood, I quietly lowered myself into a seat in the back of the auditorium. Kim stepped up to the podium and into the spotlight. She looked down at her notes. When she looked back up, she was smiling. I sighed in relief at this unexpected confidence that I would not have anticipated just months earlier.

As a student, Kim was tough in one sense and a bit too soft in another. She was self-admittedly quite shy. It was her habit to hide in a veneer of sweetness and agreeability. She was tough not because of resistance but resignation. All she wanted to out of her senior year was to finish up, graduate, and get her diploma.

The Capstone requirements and my talk about choice, learning stretch, and self-directed learning did not register with Kim. She simply could not relate. I asked about her interests in an attempt to generate ideas for a Capstone. "What do you do on your own time outside of school?" I asked.

"Paint," she said.

"Ohhh!" I said. *I didn't know she was an artist!* I jumped ahead too soon. "Can you bring in some of your work to share?" I asked.

She smiled shyly and explained, "That would be kind of hard."

"Why?" I asked.

"Well, I paint houses to help my Dad on weekends. We paint the insides, mostly. Better than sitting home alone," Kim said.

"Ohhh, I see," I said. I felt like a fool and quickly moved on.

"What else do you do?" I needed some inkling for other possibilities or directions to head in.

"I watch TV and go shopping sometimes," she answered. No leads there. Dead end. I backed off.

I sought out the art teacher for ideas. She suggested that Kim join in on a photography project that a group of students were doing outside of school. When I asked Kim if she was interested, Miss Agreeability complied. Kim met with the art teacher, received the necessary materials and instructions and scheduled a follow-up meeting. The meeting never happened. It was a no show.

At about the same time, I received a call from the elementary school physical education teacher. He was in need of someone to design and paint markers and signs for a new nature trail that meandered through school-owned land and thought it could possibly be a Capstone. I thought of Kim; *at least she would have a project.* When I asked her about it, Miss Agreeability had wised up. Kim looked down at her desk.

When looking back up at me, she winced almost as if in pain and said, "I don't think so." I backed off again.

As time ticked away, Kim did not seem bothered by the fact that she did not have a topic for her Capstone. Whenever I posed my weekly question about any new ideas, her response was always the same, a head shake "No." *Yikes! No Capstone, no cap and gown.*

In desperation, I turned to her interest in shopping. One day I saw Kim in the library; I sat down next to her and asked if she had seen the ad for a big sale at a local brand-name store. Kim lighted up. *Hey, a sign of life. Even a few sparks. Maybe we have something here.*

During our conversations, I realized what she called *shopping* was more like a hunt, an adventure, a challenge to beat limited means but still wear the highly sought-after brand-name apparel so significant to the social status of and equalizer for the adolescent. I began to notice that Kim had lots of different outfits. Each one had a story—the what, where, when, and how (much).

Back at the library table, Ashley, also a senior, sat across from Kim. Ashley was the full package: face, figure, and fashion. Ashley also had fire. She was a high achiever with a serious plan for the future. I asked Ashley where she got all her trendy, chic, and classy clothes. Pulling down her high-waisted, big-buttoned, forest-green jacket, she casually said, "Oh, I got this at Goodwill. In fact, I buy most of my clothes there. That way I always have something new. It's great. Goodwill has some real deals—high quality, vintage, and brand names."

Ashley and Kim started to talk shop about favorite stores and brands, outlets, sales, online shopping, and second hand clothing. I backed off, sat back, and just listened. Kim's voice changed from a girl's to a young woman's. She gestured with head and hands as she talked, free of self-consciousness. *So here is where she lives—in the world of fashion apparel, styles, brands, and bargains. Here was her passion.*

The girl's conversation shifted to the poor economy and the impact on the clothing market. They spoke about how second-hand stores were springing up; business was booming. Even before the economic downturn, it was *hip* to shop second-hand.

Kim's Capstone was born out of her conversation with Ashley. Kim proposed to investigate the local second-hand clothing market and analyze her findings within the context of the booming second-hand clothing business in the global market.

Kim was on it. No more prodding. While neither Kim nor I ever imagined that "shopping" might spawn a Capstone, it was not an empty topic.

Through her research, Kim learned that second-hand clothing was big business, not only at home but abroad as well, thanks to the Internet. And it was not only American teens who sought brand names and a bargain. Exports of second hand clothing from the United States did not just go to impoverished third-world countries in Central America, Asia, and Africa but also to Japan and Western Europe markets as well. Nor was it limited to charities or nonprofits. Celebrities such as Julia Roberts, Nicole Kidman, and Reese Witherspoon showed up on the red carpet in vintage gowns, and the highly publicized auctions of Jackie Kennedy Onassis' and Princess Diana's gowns made second-hand clothing a prize for the elite.

Kim also learned that second-hand clothing is hot among "green" shoppers who highly value sustainability and recycling in order to spare the landfills of discarded but reusable clothing, material, and fabrics.

Vintage and style shoppers of all ages and means seek clothing that is unavailable at retail stores. Teens in particular love to rummage through the bins and racks in search of that overlooked find buried in the rubble.

For her fieldwork, Kim compared and contrasted six area secondhand clothing stores in terms of location, hours, layout, displays, apparel, brands, type of clothing, accessories, and arrangement by size and color. Store appeal varied greatly.

The interviews with local storeowners uncovered some interesting information. Business had increased markedly since the recession. All stores sold the brand names popular among teens, their largest single group of shoppers. Markdowns varied between 25 and 60 percent of retail price.

Each owner considered her store as much a service as a business. When Kim asked about the stigma of second-hand clothing, one owner said, "I don't think it is like it used to be at all; I never used to see teenagers come in and now I do." Another owner said that since the decline in the economy, the stigma was "long gone." All owners said they only took clothes that were clean and in perfect condition. Summer wear was the most popular.

Kim was particularly struck by the connection between store appeal and sales. Second-hand shops that looked no different from any retail store, with eye-catching window displays and designer-looking decors, did the best business. Good location and convenient hours were also pluses.

Kim applied the power of visual appeal to help "sell" her Capstone presentation. The interior shots of second-hand shops that Kim used in her slideshow could easily have been taken as photos of either brand name stores or boutiques. Her portfolio was a work of art in itself—eye-catching, colorful, well organized, and professional. To authenticate the value going second-hand, Kim briefly left the stage to change into and then model onstage her figure-fitting magenta prom dress, which she had bought second-hand for just $50.

As it turned out, Kim's Capstone on second-hand clothing was highly topical. It linked together seemingly unrelated trends abuzz in the world today: the global economy, on-line buying and selling, going green, recycling, sustainability, and celebrity appeal. Second-hand clothing is a window into the world of today, merging the local with the global. Second-hand is for all ages and status. It has become a class equalizer. Most important, second-hand is not second-class.

Back in the auditorium, I settled back in my seat and relished Kim's presentation: colorful, interesting, informative, timely, and, yes, relevant. Kim had to really stretch and overcome her shyness to contact and conduct six separate interviews with storeowners. But what she was never sure she could do was her presentation. Speaking on a subject that "fit" her did the trick. Passion overruled passivity. All seniors deserve the chance to take center stage at least once—to share and be known for their passion that enlightens us with how it connects to the larger world we all share. In her reflection paper Kim wrote, "I am most proud of getting on that stage in front of people and doing my thing and showing them all that I know about this subject."

That summer my young adult daughter proudly showed off a new purchase.

"Hey Mom, how do you like my new shirt?"

"Nice. Great colors and perfect fit. Where did you get it?" I asked.

"I got it at Goodwill for a dollar," she nonchalantly said. Flipping her hair with the back of her hand, my daughter strutted off mimicking a fashion model. I just smiled and thanked Kim for enlightening me.

18

Senior Capstone

Life Related

It was a somber topic for an eighteen year old—death and dying. No one had actually died, but Emily had experienced grievous loss. As a child, she had found refuge from the turmoil at home underneath the towering evergreen trees in the countryside cemetery nearby.

For her Capstone, Emily studied the work of Elizabeth Kübler-Ross, the renowned Swiss-American psychiatrist who described the stages of grief (denial, anger, bargaining, depression, acceptance) that are normally undergone not only by those facing their own or a loved one's death but also by those who have experienced trauma or loss and are trapped in pain.

Emily used her Capstone to approach the place of acceptance regarding several unresolved relationships with family and friends. Her mentor, a counselor, supported Emily as she moved around in the stages of grief, visiting and reflecting upon her living remembrances that had made up the keys to her life and her view of herself. Emily came to realize that her visits to the place of acceptance were more like an opening than a closing. The place of acceptance had a window with a wider, more open view beyond her pain, where there was room for a fuller self—her whole Self.

To make her work tangible, Emily wrote letters. Several were never delivered but served as a safe place to say it all and then glean the essence of what she *did* need to say in person. In doing so, Emily learned that in the case of a long-lasting peer relationship, its course and ending was, to a degree, mutual. As Emily wrote in her reflection paper, this realization freed her to "*finally* move on and become someone else."

She also wrote letters of another kind, letters of appreciation and gratitude for loyal and steadfast friends. They were beautifully scribed by hand, rolled into a scroll, and tied in red bows.

Emily's Capstone presentation was "invitation-only," attended by just four of her steadfast friends along with me and another faculty member. Her presentation on the pioneering work of Kübler-Ross was powerful, and not limited to knowledge alone. By applying Kübler-Ross's work to her own life, Emily made significant strides toward healing and self-understanding. She now had a name for her pain—*grief*—which had predictable phases and places as one moves through it. Even though Emily had not fully moved into the place of acceptance, she had at least visited there and could now see a future for herself beyond home and high school.

Emily ended her journey to the place of acceptance, and her presentation, with gratitude. As a highly personal expression of this gratitude, Emily gave her friends the letters tied with red ribbons and reflected on the times and the ways her friends had shown her a wider view of life.

At the end of Emily's presentation when she and her friends had left, the other faculty member commented, "Emily clearly learned and grew a great deal from her Capstone, but I don't really see how it is school-related." I said nothing, but mentally replied, "Better than that, it is *life-related*."

Emily wrote in her Capstone Reflection Paper, "I believe that it is one of the greatest achievements I've made in my lifetime, and I'm glad I had the opportunity [to] do it. I expect to reserve my new knowledge for times when I really need it . . . in times when growth is necessary, and maturity is required."

Part VI

Unleashed to Teach

A Glimpse Inside a
21st Century Classroom

19

Both Sides of the Coin

On the first day of class of a new school year, I pose two seemingly obvious questions to the incoming seniors.

First question—"How many students in this room?"

The still compliant, fresh-to-the-new-year students gaze around the room counting heads.

"Eighteen," says one student matter-of-factly.

I say nothing, pause, and move on to the second question. "How many teachers in this room?"

Another student says nonchalantly, "One."

I can sense the students think I am establishing my role as ruler of the class, top dog, the alpha. Again, I say nothing. Pause.

I repeat the question more slowly and softly this time, "How many *teachers* in this room?"

The students furrow their brows. Some look down uncomfortably while others gaze around the room searching for clues.

"Ah, I get it," answers a student finally. "Nineteen teachers. We're all teachers. Right?"

I smile and nod in agreement. "Okay, then how many *students* in this room?"

Silence. At last, some brave soul tentatively asks, "Nineteen?"

Again, I smile. Taking a quarter from my pants pocket, I start tossing it in the air. "Student and teacher are the flip side of the same coin. One cannot exist without the other." I toss the quarter one last time. "Student or teacher?"

There is the co-existence of both student and teacher whether undertaking or facilitating a Capstone. Ultimately the student completes his Capstone by becoming a teacher to his school community.

20

Double H Double J

Students love classroom rituals. It makes them feel that their particular class is special, a kind of club. One of the seniors' favorites was dubbed "Double H, Double J," short for "Happy-Happy-Joy-Joy." DHDJ was created as a spontaneous community builder at the beginning of the school year, but the students insisted that it continue all year long, right up to graduation. Each new week began with a quick round of DHDJ, one positive per person, all within no more than ten minutes. The positive could be as monumental as defeating the rival soccer team or as ordinary as a pizza party and movie on Saturday night. On the occasion when I tried to forego DHDJ due to time restraints, I had an outright rebellion on my hands.

We all recognized the value of the DHDJ ritual—an opportunity for each and every person to be seen and heard. Classmates across the room who seemingly had nothing in common would share a laugh, make affirming comments— "Cool!" "Awesome!" "Sweet!" Or my favorite—"That is so sick!" During DHDJ, students shared their common culture— the latest movie such as *Avatar*, or the *Twilight* book series, or the new underage dance club in town. On occasion, a student needed to share the downside—an illness, disappointment, or loss. At these times I knew a high level of trust had developed. The class had transformed into a community, a safe haven where they could share the load.

It was my intention for DHDJ to help the students transition from the weekend back to school and to create a positive frame of mind and good vibe in the space that we shared together. In time, the weekly DHDJ ritual transformed a class into a mini-community.

The Senior Capstone became a strong community builder within the classroom, the school and its community.

21

Give Me Oxygen!

It hits me every time I attend a conference. It starts to happen about 10:30 a.m. and by 4:00 p.m. I could either scream or I am falling asleep.

After I return from the conference, I ask my students how they do it day after day.

"What?" they ask.

"Sit," I say.

I ask myself, *How can we expect students to be engaged, energized, and focused when they sit for extended periods with only five minutes to pass between classes?* Humans were built to be movers, not sitters. We are bipedalers, not bottom-sitters. Most high school students do not even get to go outside during the day unless they attend a school with an open campus.

When a student sits too long, blood settles into his seat and is not circulating in his brain. To get blood back into circulation, the body needs to move. In addition to oxygen, the brain needs nutrition, hydration, stimulation, and relaxation.

Ironically, adult learning environments such as those found in higher education and at professional conferences are often more brain-friendly than schools for children with growing brains.

Without the standard conference comforts, no one would attend. There are 15-minute breaks between hour-long sessions with nourishing food and beverages to refuel. There are no restrictions on bathrooms breaks. One can walk around freely in common areas to stretch, or even go outside to catch some rays and fresh air. The more dynamic presenters always have activities to get participants interacting and moving. Lunch breaks are at least an hour and sometimes longer.

I remember college as such a relief. There was no more herding or feeling clamped down. Scenic walks across campus recharged the battery and brain. Exercise facilities were open all day and night. Today, colleges know that fitness and student centers must be state-of-the-art to attract applicants.

During my first two years of teaching in high school, I was in a "portable" sandwiched between the main building and the track that was surrounded by a nature conservancy. On beautiful fall and spring days, my classes would take a ten-minute walk around the track for a break during the 80-minute class period. (The boys always ran lapping the girls three to one.) "Ahhh." Air. Sunlight. Soft breeze. Smell of pine. We had to be quiet and careful not to call attention to ourselves. I kept the windows and back door that looked out onto the playing fields open as long as possible in the fall and reopened them as soon as possible in the spring.

Students were permitted to chew gum, doodle, or stand in the back of the class in order to keep some part of their bodies in motion and thereby their brain as well. The class took stretch breaks. Rather than go hungry with no fuel for the brain, students were allowed to eat discretely their breakfast, lunch, or snack. Drinking water was encouraged to keep the brain hydrated, but I'll admit they preferred sports drinks. Those who fidgeted got foam-rubber squeeze balls to channel their energy. There were plants in the room, and the harsh, buzzing fluorescent lights overhead were turned off.

We had the brain covered: oxygen, hydration, nutrition, stimulation, and relaxation.

The Capstone frees students to learn outside the confines of the classroom where they can oxygenate in the air or water, on the field or trail, in a workshop, studio, or laboratory. Oxygenation of the body and brain is essential for learning at full capacity.

22

Zapped by a Zamboni

Sam and his partner modeled their Capstone after the MTV show *The Buried Life*, in which a group of young adults travel the country in a bus to fulfill their Life List: "100 Things to Do Before I Die." Driving a Zamboni was an item on Sam's Life List.

To my mind, a Life List is a great idea for Senior Capstone—a personal guide for one's life with goals and direction. Why waste time?

As a former rink mom, I frequently witnessed Zamboni magic, the transformation of a cut-up, roughed-up, ice-shaved surface into clear, smooth glass. To glide over "zambonified" ice was close to the feeling of flying.

Call it familiarity or nostalgia, I was most enthused about Sam's Zamboni idea. This was a great kick-off to Sam's Life List Capstone. It was doable. A faculty member whose son was the manager of the local ice arena thought driving the Zamboni could be arranged. It would probably be exhilarating, close to the feeling of flying.

Every week for a month, I asked Sam if he had called the local ice arena. "No, not yet," was always the answer. As the end of the ice hockey season grew near, I became concerned about the window of opportunity for the Zamboni.

At the beginning of class one morning, I asked Sam to step out in the hall and call the ice arena on his cell phone. When Sam came back to class, he said, "There was no answer; it must not be open yet." I was puzzled. I knew the ice arena opened very early in the morning. Between classes, *I* called. Sure enough, they answered. The rink was closing for the spring season in two days. There was no time left for Sam to learn to drive the Zamboni.

During a free period, I called Sam into my room for a chat. Without sharing the bad news, I asked why he had been so resistant to calling the ice arena when he had a connection there and had been so excited about driving the Zamboni. He pulled a chair up to my desk, straddled it backwards, and crossed his arms over the backrest. He lowered his head, looked at the floor, and spoke his truth. "Because, Mrs. Aronson, *you* were so excited about the Zamboni and on me so much about it, you took it away from me; it became your thing, not mine."

"Oh," I said. Lesson learned. *Huge* lesson learned. You can support, guide, encourage, and advise but must not get too close. Rightly so, students will resist and pull away. They may even sit back and let you do it. Rather than fight, they will just give it to you, let you take ownership because you seem to want it so much. Whenever I resorted to force or control in my role as facilitator of the Capstone, I got *zapped* every time.

Well, Sam's level of honesty certainly cleared the ice. Meanwhile, Sam did get to fly for the first time in his life, another item on his Life List—not across the ice but across the sky with an alumnus who had obtained his pilot's license for his Senior Capstone.

Ownership by the student is a key factor for success with the Capstone. Outside interference by way of force or control can zap the life out of it.

23

Looping

It's 5:00 am. I wearily open the manila folder and pull out the top essay from the stack as I try to shake off the sleep in my head with another sip of fresh brewed coffee. Caffeine aside, I am in for a wake-up call.

Seeing John's name, I loosen my editing grip. Sure enough, the essay is well-crafted. It is clean, with no technical errors. I make a few comments in the margins and top it off with an A. Done. Next! I hurry to review a couple more essays before heading to school.

At the end of class, I hand back the personal essays usable for college applications. I tell the students that their grade is a preliminary one and suggest that they make revisions based on my feedback. John is the last to get his essay back. He ignores his grade but tilts his head to read the feedback written in the margins. Class is over and the students hit the hall.

John does not stir from his seat. Looking down at his essay he mutters, "Ah . . ." I move closer and wait to hear more. *This can't be about the grade—he got an A.* The last of the caffeine kicks in.

Looking up from his paper, John says, "I still want to work on this. . . . I might use it for my college essay. . .How can I make it better?"

"Well, let's see," I offer. I take another look at his essay. I had made a few suggestions for word choice and syntax but basically left his essay intact. *Was I settling for good-enough, even on the best essay in the class?*

Back to John. He wants more. I *tweaked* his essay. He wants me to *work* it. John is a state champion in cross-country. He does not settle for less than the best.

"Let me take another look and I'll get back to you next class," I finally say.

John is satisfied. He turns to call "Thanks" over his shoulder as he vanishes out the doorway.

At lunch, I eat alone in my classroom and take another pass at his essay. After looking it over several times, I start to rip it apart like a hungry editor. After all, he did give me permission. How far should I go? You have to tread lightly with personal essays. *Don't mess with their self-esteem.* It is safe to stick with matters of language. I stop. *What does the perfect-scorer-on-the-AP-English-exam-and-best-writer-in-the-entire-school-hands-down-by-faculty-consensus want from me?* I suspect that what he wants is more specific feedback— possible ways to make his essay a real standout and en-*courage*-ment to dig deeper, to get more traction. Okay then, I will need courage too when I see him next class.

John shyly hangs back at the end of class. I smile and pull out his essay from my manila folder. John holds the paper close to his face as he tries to decipher my hard-to-read notes in the margins of his essay. I explain: Mix up the chronology so it's not so linear. No problem there. Done. He also agrees it's a bit sappy. This is remedied by more show, less tell. Alter sentence structure here and there and add some dialogue. No sweat. He is still with me so I go to center sun and hope I don't get burned.

"Although your essay is well written, it does not do you justice," I tell John. "Where is the John I know? This essay represents a younger version of yourself, not who you have become. Don't short-change yourself. Your humility is dousing your intensity. Write like you run. Kick up some heat."

Stunned, John's eyes widen and look straight into mine. "Oh."

"Look it over at lunch so you can chew on it," I advise. "See what you can do and we'll talk after class."

We volley back and forth over several more revisions. The volley is energizing. We work together in a system of feedback—that is, we form a feedback loop. There is life in it. John asks me not to stop at *A*: this was for college admissions. It is real-world, not for a grade in school.

John comes through with a real goosebumps essay, one that evokes strong feeling. Yes, it is beautifully written and comes from his center sun.

Grades are a closed system. Grades end or shut down the conversation, the exchange between student and teacher. Feedback opens it up. Feedback, by definition, is a loop. In fact, all the systems of our body operate using feedback loops. Our life depends on it. If even one feedback loop in our system shuts down, that will be the end. No life. Biomimicry looks to nature for models of efficacy. If a system has sustained life through millennia, why not use that as a model, even in education?

The volley of feedback between student and teacher keeps learning alive. It is how the game is supposed to be played.

Feedback was the most effective means for guiding students through the self-designed and full circle learning process of the Capstone.

24

Backpacks as Vestige

Backpacks are bad for the spine and, I contend, the brain. Recent research has shown that school backpacks cause back pain, spinal asymmetries and disc displacement in children.[1] Aside from the measurable harm, it is an image of burden, of being weighed down. Hopefully, backpacks will very soon be a vestige of the past.

So what is in those bulging bags? Not just books but *textbooks* that have become big and heavy from the thickening of knowledge. Textbooks may have their place but not on students' backs. Textbooks do not always carry their own weight. They are costly, only partially used, get damaged or lost, take space to store, and are soon outdated.

A 2012 science textbook shelved in my home as reference has 1,077 pages excluding glossary and index. It weighs 5.2 lbs and measures 9 by 11 inches—nothing I would want to carry on my back all day. Granted, the colored illustrations, diagrams, photos on glossy paper help balance out the hard to read 10 pt. print.

The content of textbooks is compacted knowledge compiled and edited from sources several times removed. The writing can be dry and dense, the wording confounding, and the relevance and meaning hard to determine. Do I hear a brain scream? The so-called fruit of knowledge has already been selected, picked, processed and packaged. All the students need to do is eat and try their best to digest.

There is an ingenious new trend, however, in the textbook industry. Teachers can now customize and construct their textbooks from a selection of chapters or content options. Textbooks are now digitalized and interactive. The industry is catching on.

Sound facetious? Well, okay I'll admit it. I had textbook envy at times—the complete all-in-one-course-book—the full package: teacher's manual, instruction guide, outlined chapters, suggested learning activities, experiments or problems, summaries, review, and test questions. Needless to say, there was no textbook for the Capstone.

Back to the backpack. The students' most valued possessions in their backpacks are the most mobile and lightweight— cell phone and laptop. Essentially, all else can go. If all those oversized, thick and heavy textbooks were dropped, it would be a real load off everyone's backs. Students of today need school to reflect the real world. Tools for learning need to be mobile, high speed, multi-media, and customized.

I say get off students' backs and lighten the load with light touch. The new "backpack" will be as light as an iPad. Currently, high schools are loading textbooks onto iPads. This is a step in the right direction in terms of the back. Soon students will be able to walk again with backs straight and shoulders square.

But what about the brain? Could it be that pre-packaged information and knowledge take the fun out of learning? Can we really expect textbooks to evoke curiosity, inquiry, engagement, let alone a love of learning? What about the search for and discernment of information and knowledge on a primary and secondary level?

Textbooks do have a place in the classroom—on the shelf. They can be used as a quick, comprehensive reference or a kind of encyclopedia on a given subject. Note that textbooks are not considered a legitimate source for citing research—the content is at least once removed from its original source.

Fruit freshly picked is much more succulent than the fruit long removed from its stem-source despite the glossy packaged appearance in the store. So shelve those textbooks, at least some of the time. Dare to be textbook-free, at least some of the time, and give students' backs and brains relief, at least some of the time.

For the Capstone, primary sources of information and knowledge from direct experience, experimentation, investigation, or communication with experts and mentors was the preferred method of research and learning. This was supplemented with secondary sources found in print or media. Discernment of the quality, value, and relevance of a source was part of the learning process.

25

To Hit Your Mark...
Open Your Heart

Suzanne, our facilitator at a leadership workshop for women, was a formidable teacher even though she had never formally studied pedagogy or instructional methodologies. She spoke few words, just enough to guide us through an activity using instruction, observation, and feedback. Embodying all that she taught, she took each of us, the workshop participants, to our self-imposed limit and then beyond it. She knew how learning happens: *doing* leads to experience. Meaningful experience requires reflection and integration—and under her guidance, we did each in turn.

The three-day workshop was filled with one challenging activity after another. The most powerful was archery. No one in our group of forty had any experience in archery—we were all novices. I suspect that is one reason this activity was chosen. After reviewing safety rules and cautioning us that we were in possession of an instrument that could do serious harm, Suzanne gave us clear instructions and a demonstration on how to stand, set the bow, aim, and release. We each shot three rounds of eight arrows.

As we clumsily fumbled with the unfamiliar equipment and attempted to set the bow, Suzanne made some observations: "Some of you over-analyze and try to figure out how it all works before you will take aim and release. Archery is not done with the head but with the heart. If you hesitate too long after setting your bow, it will start to shake, you will lose power, and the arrow will fall short. If you lean away from your target, you are pulling back in fear and you'll lose power. If you lean in too much, you are forcing it, and you will miss your mark.

"Ground yourself firmly with shoulders squarely over hips. Find your spot on the target. Focus there, empty your mind and be one with the bow, arrow, and your spot. Stretch the bow fully with an even push/pull and open your heart. *To hit your mark, you must open your heart.*"

It was breathtaking to see Suzanne take the archer's pose, eye the target, set her bow with an even, steady pull, and release eight arrows in rapid succession, hitting near the center of the target every time. She did not do it to show off, but to give us a picture of the posture, timing, and rhythm.

When my turn came, I hit just outside the bull's-eye with the first arrow. Cheers went up behind the line. *How did I do that?* I was befuddled. *Beginner's luck?* I could not account for my performance.

Successive shots were off the mark or did not even hit the target. I was in my head, trying too hard to replicate the performance of my initial shot. I became flustered and self-conscious and ended back at fumbling with the bow and arrow. From behind the line I heard Suzanne repeat, *"To hit your mark, you must open your heart."*

The group of forty novice archers had varying degrees of success. Only one arrow hit the bull's-eye; about half hit somewhere on or near the target.

For the final round, Suzanne instructed us to write an important personal goal on a piece of paper and attach it to the target. Everyone proceeded to attach her goal to the center of the target, right over the bull's-eye. Everyone except Cynthia—she attached her goal high, above the target and onto the bale of hay that the target was mounted on. Cynthia was the only one to hit her goal—a bull's-eye, right into the hay. Her goal was to *raise* funds for the victims of the Haitian earthquake.

A sobering silence fell over the group. Everyone looked to Suzanne for her reaction. She just stood holding her bow at her side, smiled, and nodded knowingly. I repeated her words so not to forget: *To hit your mark, you must open your heart . . .* and aim high where your arrows fly.

The Capstone must be done with as much heart as head to lift off the ground and fly. Capstones done with heart reach, come close, or pass straight through the students' mark.

Last Words

The Capstone program came full circle for me at my farewell bonfire with former students from across the six years, now all alumni. By the end of the evening, the bonfire had burned to embers, empty soda cans were strewn on the ground, pictures had been taken and snacks consumed.

Ben, one of the last to leave, backslapped his departing friends good-bye and gave me a final hug. I watched him turn and start the climb up the hill towards the street and to his car. In the silhouette of night, Ben appeared to be a man, no longer a boy. He was a big, strong guy, but he did not use his size to push his weight around. Rather, he had that young adult way of rounding his shoulders slightly, looking down, and putting his hands in his pockets when sharing his thoughts.

When halfway up the hill, Ben turned slightly to look back behind him through the darkness. The moonlight caught the side of his face. He startled slightly when he saw that I was just a few feet behind him. Catching my eyes, he said, "You brought out the best in me." He then turned, put his hands in his pockets, looked down, and headed back up the hill to his car.

Those were the last words that I would hear from a freshly graduated senior. For a moment I stopped midway up the hill and said nothing; there was no need for a reply. But I thought to myself, *No, I just asked the question, 'What do you want to learn?' and then held the space for you to do just that.*

Ben was the rightful spokesman for the Capstone. Our dance together as student and teacher had been like so many others before him. The initial overconfidence as a defense, the struggle to choose and scope out a Capstone topic, the apprehension about contacting a mentor, the tendency towards procrastination, the reluctance to reach out for help when stuck, the push towards completion and success, and the final and frequently heard expression of empowering growth: "I never knew it was in me; I never knew I could do it."

Earlier that final spring, I had had a dream in which I was holding a "baby" that I had nurtured and raised but was ready to pass on to another who knew how to raise it to its next stage of development and who would love it as I had. This dream of passing on "my baby," the Capstone, to a full-capacity successor came true, as did my first dream six years earlier. It was my dream to reach what was best in students not in terms of a grade but in terms of their particular brand of genius accessed through learning at full capacity.

The final results of the Capstones were not always finely packaged or polished. Some seniors never really got on board and others fell short. But more often than not, students reached into their core and stretched themselves to learn at a fuller capacity.

Yes, it was stressful at times for them to take on this level of responsibility and accountability for one's own learning—to shift from being a passive to an active learner. Not so much because of the work involved but because it was their "baby," their responsibility. But when students did make the shift, it was truly empowering.

One former student contacted me via Facebook to share the joy of receiving the Communication Sciences and Disorders Senior Capstone Award for her college research on the early detection of autism. As a high school student, she struggled and then stretched to clear some of the same hurdles mentioned above. For her high school Capstone she built a hope chest as a family heirloom. The difference between her high school and college Capstones could not have been more different. But that is irrelevant. Rather it was the *process*—both the scope and the challenge to learn and create beyond what might seem possible—that she expressed appreciation for in her Facebook message:

I thought I'd let you know that looking back I'm glad I had a Capstone experience prior to college. I really appreciate your drive to push us to do something "big" and your support throughout the process . . . . I wanted to share that with you and let you know that your influence on me to create something "big" has stayed with me throughout my college Capstone experience. . . .

Last words.

Afterword

Self-Designed Learning: A Growing Option in Higher Education

Self-designed, experiential, and interdisciplinary education is in the wings of secondary and higher education ready to move to center stage. The time has come for students, with guidance, to be the designers and directors of their own course of study in, at least, the upper levels of high school and higher education. It is an encouraging sign that a significant number of high schools and colleges now require a Senior Project or Capstone as a graduation requirement for a diploma, specific major, or degree.

Similarly, individualized and interdisciplinary majors are growing in popularity. College students can either design their course of study through an individualized major or can at least combine fields of study through the interdisciplinary major. The interdisciplinary major option in high education has tripled to well over a thousand in the last decade.[1] Interdisciplinarity is one of the "catch fire" ideas for 21st century liberal arts education [2] However, these options to design one's own course of study are not widely known or publicized within universities. Dan Gordon, professor of history and associate dean of the Commonwealth Honors College at the University of Massachusetts Amherst believes that the main obstacle for the individualized major is the organization of large universities into specialized disciplines.[3] It is astounding to realize that the overall structure of departments and disciplines within the university has remained mostly unchanged for over 100 years.[4] Yet the growing popularity and probable demand for these self-designed options for learning in college suggest that students want their education to more closely align with their greatest interests, aspirations for the future, and the world they will enter after college.

Robert J. Sternberg, professor of psychology and dean of the School of Arts and Sciences at Tufts University contends, "The current idea of a major (or minor) may have made more sense in a less complex and interconnected world . . ." An advocate of interdisciplinary problem-based learning, Sternberg questions whether undergraduates educated in the major/minor system are taught to think in ways that prepare them for the problems they will face once they leave the college environment.[5]

To study the outcomes for graduates who chose and then created an interdisciplinary or individualized course of study would be the subject of another whole book. But if the individualized major at UMass Amherst called Bachelor's Degree with Individual Concentration (BDIC) is any indication, the effects of designing one's course of study are powerful and even transformational. At the 2011 BDIC graduation, Gordon spoke of the new UMass BDIC graduates as leaders, innovators, creators, entrepreneurs, and activists. "They did not pick a major off the shelf but built a new shelf. They did not just create a major, but created a life," said Gordon. It's widely recognized on campus that BDIC graduates are among the university's most successful professionals.[6]

In this age of creative economy, it is both practical and empowering for students to design their own course of study. It is practical as the best value for the investment of time and money spent on education—both being at a premium for students of the twenty-first century. It is empowering because students can align knowledge and its application with their core interests and aspirations as they learn and create at full capacity to set a direction for their lives with purpose and meaning. Is that not the highest calling of education?

$\mathcal{E}ndnotes$

Introduction and Background

1. Definition of "genius" in Merriam-webster.com, accessed 12 June 2012.
2. See bibliography for books by Howard Gardner, especially *Multiple Intelligences: New Horizons* and *Multiple Intelligences: The Theory in Practice.*
3. See bibliography for books by Daniel Goleman: *Emotional Intelligence* and *Social Intelligence.*
4. See bibliography for sources on brain development and brain-based learning: Eric P. Jensen, *Brain-Based Learning* and *Teaching with the Brain in Mind*; and Renate N. Caine and G. Caine, *Making Connections*; R. M. C. deCharms, "Christopher deCharms Looks Inside the Brain," M. I. Posner and M. K. Rothbart, *Educating the Human Brain.* Richard Restak, *The New Brain: How the Modern Age Is Rewiring Your Mind* and *The Secret Life of the Brain*; David A. Sousa, *How the Brain Learns*; Rita Smilkstein, *We're Born to Learn*; Robert Sylwester, *A Celebration of Neurons*; and James E. Zull, *The Art of Changing the Brain.*
5. Parker Palmer and Arthur Zajonc, *The Heart of Higher Education: A Call to Renewal* (San Francisco: Jossey-Bass, 2010), 61.
6. Doc Lew Childre and Howard Martin, *The HeartMath Solution* (New York: HarperCollins, 1999).
7. Stephen Harrod Buhner, *The Intelligence of the Heart: The Secret Teachings of Plants in the Direct Perception of Nature* (Rochester, VT: Bear and Company, 2004), 97–105.
8. Karen Custer, *Care and Feeding of the Energetic Core* (Bloomington, IN: AuthorHouse, 2005), 118.

9. Greg Whitby, "Twenty-First-Century Pedagogy" (video), 29 September 2007, www.youtube.com/watch?v=l72UFXqa8ZU, accessed 16 April 2011.

Innate Intelligence and Learning to Create

1. Robert Fritz, *The Path of Least Resistance: The Principles of Creating What You Want to Create* (Salem, MA: Stillpoint Publishing Company, 1984), 25–46.
2. Ibid., 47.
3. Ken Robinson, *Out of Our Minds: Learning to Be Creative* (Oxford, UK: Capstone Publishing Limited, 2001); Ken Robinson and Lou Aronica, *The Element: How Finding Your Passion Changes Everything* (New York: Viking, 2009).
4. Ken Robinson, "Do Schools Kill Creativity?" (TED Talk video), January 6, 2007, www.youtube.com/watch?v=iG9CE55wbtY, accessed December 7, 2011; Sir Ken Robinson, "Bring on the Learning Revolution!" (TED Talk video), May 2010, www.ted.com/talks/sir_ken_robinson_bring_on_the_revolution.html, accessed 7 December 2011.
5. Robinson, *Out of Our Minds*, 114.
6. Ibid., 115.
7. Owen Boss, "New Law Aims to Measure School Creativity," *Daily Hampshire Gazette*, August 8, 2010.
8. Ibid.
9. Chad Cain, "Hampshire Starts Center for Creativity," *Daily Hampshire Gazette*, 21 October 2011, A1, B2.
10. See: www.hampshire.edu/news/Hampshire-College-Establishes-Creativity-Center.htm, "Hampshire College Establishes Creativity Center."

Shift in Six

1. Anne Fadiman, *The Spirit Catches You and You Fall Down: A Hmong Child, Her American Doctors, and the Collision of Two Cultures* (New York: Farrar, Straus, and Giroux, 1997).

The Capstone Model for Learning in the Twenty-First Century

1. Confucius quotes: www.brainyquote.com/quotes/authors/c/confucius.html, accessed 2 February 2011.
2. Osho Zen Ta quote: http://oshoonline.blogspot.com/2010/03/you-are-not-accidental-existence-needs.html, accessed 12 May 2011.
3. Seventh Generation Education, *The Library of Halexandriah* (n.d.), http://halexandria.org/dward038.htm, accessed 3 March 2011.
4. See: Merriam-Webster's *Third New International Dictionary of the English Language*, 1961.

Power at the Core

1. Michael D. Gershon, *The Second Brain* (New York: HarperCollins, 1998).

The Diamond

1. Gary Hawkins, "Field of Dreams: In the Field," *Kennebec Journal Morning Sentinel,* 3 June 2006, IC.

Release of the Beast

1. *The Automosextacycle* by livinonluckk (video), 23 May 2008, www.youtube.com/watch?v=adwDazJg9jM, accessed: 8 January 8, 2011.

Out of Time

1. Ronald Mallet, *Time Traveler: A Scientist's Personal Mission to Make Time Travel a Reality* (New York: Thunder's Mouth Press, 2006).

Saturated by Silence

1. Jennifer Roback Morse, "Good Sex: Why We Need More of It and a Lot Less of the Bad Stuff," (*American Enterprise*, April 2006), 18–29.

A Serious Business

1. Norman Cousins, *Anatomy of an Illness as Perceived by the Patient: Reflections on Healing and Regeneration* (New York: Bantam Books, 1979).

Backpacks as Vestige

1. T.B. Neuschwander, et al. "The effect of backpacks on the lumbar spine of children: A Standing magnetic resonance imaging study," (*Spine Journal*, 35, no.1 (2010), 83-88.

Afterword: Self-Designed Education

1. Robert K. Elder, "Designer Majors: Rise in Interdisciplinary Study Programs Reflects Career, Cultural Changes," *Chicago Tribune*, 26 February 2007, www.highbeam.com/doc/1G1-159793993.html, accessed 19 July 2012.
2. Diane Ravitch et al. "Interdisciplinary Education at Liberal Arts Institutions." *Teagle Foundation White Paper*. New York: Teagle Foundation, n.d. www.evergreen.edu/washcenter/resources/upload/2006ssrc whitepaper.pdf, accessed 21 March 2012.
3. Dan Gordon, personal communication, 8 August 2011.

4. Andrew Abbott, *Chaos of Disciplines* (Chicago: University of Chicago Press, 2001), 122.
5. Robert J. Sternberg, "Interdisciplinary Problem-Based Learning: An Alternative to Traditional Majors and Minors," *Liberal Education* 94, no. 1 (2008), 12–17, www.aacu.org/liberaleducation/le-wi08/le-wi08_inter_prob.cfm, accessed 22 January, 2011.
6. Dan Gordon, ibid.

Bibliography

Abbott, Andrew. *Chaos of Disciplines.* Chicago: University of Chicago Press, 2001.

Abdallah, Jameelah. "Lowering Teacher Attrition Rates through Collegiality." *Academic Leadership Journal* 7, no. 1 (2009). www.academicleadership.org/article/lowering-teacher-attrition-rates-through-collegiality.

Ackroyd, Judith. *Role Reconsidered: A Re-evaluation of the Relationship between Teacher-in-Role and Acting.* Stoke-on-Trent. UK: Trentham, 2004.

Alsop, Ron. *The Trophy Kids Grow Up: How the Millennial Generation Is Shaking Up the Workplace.* San Francisco, CA: Jossey-Bass, 2008.

Arends, Richard, and Ann Kilcher. *Teaching for Student Learning: Becoming an Accomplished Teacher.* New York: Routledge, 2010.

Armstrong, Thomas. *Multiple Intelligences in the Classroom,* 2nd ed. Alexandria, VA: Association for Supervision and Curriculum Development, 2000.

Arnold, K. D. *Lives of Promise: What Becomes of High School Valedictorians: A Fourteen-Year Study of Achievement and Life Choices.* San Francisco, CA: Jossey-Bass, 1995.

Atwater, P. M. H. *Children of the New Millennium: Children's Near-Death Experiences and the Evolution of Humankind.* New York: Three Rivers, 1999.

———. *Beyond the Indigo Children: The New Children and the Coming of the Fifth World.* Rochester, VT: Bear & Company, 2005.

Babbage, Keen J. *Extreme Teaching*. Lanham, MD: Scarecrow
    Press, 2002.
Bellanca, James A., and Ronald S. Brandt. *21st Century Skills:
    Rethinking How Students Learn*. Bloomington, IN:
    Solution Tree, 2010.
Berk, Ronald A. *Humor as an Instructional Defibrillator:
    Evidence-Based Techniques in Teaching and
    Assessment*. Sterling, VA: Stylus Publishing, 2002.
Blumberg, Phyllis. *Developing Learner-Centered Teaching: A
    Practical Guide for Faculty*. San Francisco, CA:
    Jossey-Bass, 2009.
Boss, Owen. "New Law Aims to Measure School Creativity."
    Daily Hampshire Gazette, 18 August 2010.
Buhner, Stephen Harrod. *The Secret Teachings of Plants: The
    Intelligence of the Heart in the Direct Perception of
    Nature*. Rochester, VT: Bear & Company, 2004.
Cain, Chad. "Hampshire Starts Center for Creativity." *Daily
    Hampshire Gazette*, 21 October 2011, A1, B2.
Caine, Renate N., and G. Caine. *Making Connections:
    Teaching and the Human Brain*. Alexandria, VA:
    Association for Supervision and Curriculum
    Development, 1991.
———. *The Brain, Education, and the Competitive Edge*.
    Lanham, MD: Rowman & Littlefield Education, 2001.
Carew, T. J., and S. H. Magsamen. "Neuroscience and
    Education: An Ideal Partnership for Producing
    Evidence-Based Solutions to Guide 21st Century
    Learning." *Neuron* 67, no. 5 (1 January 2001): 685–8.
Childre, Doc Lew, and Howard Martin. *The HeartMath
    Solution*. New York: HarperCollins, 1999.
Church, Dawson. *The Genie in Your Genes: Epigenetic
    Medicine and the New Biology of Intention*. Santa Rosa,
    CA: Energy Psychology Press, 2009.
Claxton, George W. "Summit to Explore Creative Economy."
    Daily Hampshire Gazette, 14 March 2011, C1–C2.

Collins, Allan, and Richard Halverson. *Rethinking Education in the Age of Technology: The Digital Revolution and Schooling in America*. New York: Teachers College Press, 2009.

Cooksy, L. "Challenges and Opportunities in Experiential Learning." *American Journal of Evaluation* 29, no. 3 (January 2008): 340–42.

Cousins, Norman. *Anatomy of an Illness as Perceived by the Patient: Reflections on Healing and Regeneration*. New York: Bantam Books, 1979.

Cox, Lee Ann. "The Senior Project." *University of Vermont Quarterly* 57 (2010): 26–33.

Custer, Karen. *Care and Feeding of the Energetic Core*. Bloomington, IN: Authorhouse, 2005.

Davis, A. J. "The Credentials of Brain-Based Learning." *Journal of Philosophy of Education* 38, no. 1 (February 2004).

Deal, Terry E., and Peggy D. Redman. *Reviving the Soul of Teaching: Balancing Metrics and Magic*. Thousand Oaks, CA: Corwin Press, 2009.

deCharms, Christopher. "Christopher deCharms Looks Inside the Brain" (Video file). February 2008. www.ted.com/talks/christopher_decharms_scans_the_brain_in_real_time.html.

DeGrandpre, Richard. *Ritalin Nation: Rapid-Fire Culture and the Transformation of Human Consciousness*. New York: W. W. Norton & Co., 1999.

Diller, Lawrence H. *Remembering Ritalin: A Doctor and Generation Rx Reflect on Life and Psychiatric Drugs*. New York: Penguin Group, 2011.

Doyle, Terry. *Helping Students Learn in a Learner-Centered Environment: A Guide to Facilitating Learning in Higher Education*. Sterling, VA: Stylus Publishing, 2008.

Easton, Freda. "Educating the Whole Child, 'Head, Heart, and Hands': Learning from the Waldorf Experience." *Theory into Practice* 36, no. 2 (1997): 87.

Elder, Robert K. "Designer Majors: Rise in Interdisciplinary Study Programs Reflects Career, Cultural Changes." *Chicago Tribune*, 26 February 2007. www.highbeam.com/doc/1G1-159793993.html.

Engel, Susan. "Let Kids Rule the School." *New York Times*, 14 March 2011. www.nytimes.com/2011/03/15/opinion/15engel.html?_r =1&scp=1&sq=Let%20Kids%20Rule%20the%20Scho ol&st=Search.

Fadiman, Anne. *The Spirit Catches You and You Fall Down: A Hmong Child, Her American Doctors, and the Collision of Two Cultures*. New York: Farrar, Straus, and Giroux, 1997.

Field, Tiffany. *Touch*. Cambridge, MA: MIT Press, 2001.

Fioriello, P. "4 Reasons Why Teachers Leave the Profession." *Online Education Consultant*, 3 March 2011. drpfconsults.com/4-real-reasons-why-teachers-leave-the-profession/.

Florida, Richard. *The Rise of the Creative Class: And How It's Transforming Work, Leisure, Community, and Everyday Life*. New York: Basic Books, 2002.

Fogarty, Robin, and Judy Stoehr. *Integrating Curricula with Multiple Intelligences: Teams, Themes, and Threads*. Thousand Oaks, CA: Corwin Press, 2008.

Fritz, Robert. *The Path of Least Resistance: The Principles of Creating What You Want to Create*. Salem, MA: Stillpoint Publishing Company, 1984.

Gamerman, Ellen. "What Makes Finnish Kids So Smart?" *Wall Street Journal*, 7 November 2011. online.wsj.com/article/SB120425355065601997.html

Gardner, Howard. *Five Minds for the Future*. Boston: Harvard Business School Press, 2006.

———. *Multiple Intelligences: New Horizons.* New York: BasicBooks, 2006.

———. *Multiple Intelligences: The Theory in Practice.* New York: BasicBooks, 1993.

———. *The Unschooled Mind: How Children Think and How Schools Should Teach.* New York: BasicBooks, 1991.

Gatto, John Taylor. *Dumbing Us Down: The Hidden Curriculum of Compulsory Schooling.* Philadelphia: New Society, 1992.

Gatto, John Taylor. *Weapons of Mass Instruction: A Schoolteacher's Journey through the Dark World of Compulsory Schooling.* Gabriola Island, BC: New Society, 2010.

Gershon, Michael D. *The Second Brain.* New York: HarperCollins, 1998.

Gigerenzer, Gerd. *Gut Feelings: The Intelligence of the Unconscious.* New York: Viking Penguin, 2007.

Gladwell, Malcolm. *The Tipping Point: How Little Things Can Make a Big Difference.* New York: Little, Brown & Company, 2000.

———. *Blink: The Power of Thinking.* New York: Little Brown & Company, 2005.

———. *Outliers: The Story of Success.* New York: Little, Brown & Company, 2008.

Goleman, Daniel. *Emotional Intelligence: Why It Can Matter More than IQ.* New York: Bantam Books, 1995.

———. *Social Intelligence: The New Science of Human Relationships.* New York: Bantam Books, 2006.

Goswami, U. "Neuroscience and Education: From Research to Practice?" *Neuroscience* 7, no. 5 (January 2006): 406–11.

Grossberg, Stephen. "The Link between Brain Learning, Attention, and Consciousness." *Consciousness and Cognition* 8, no. 1 (1 March 1999).

Hart, Tobin. *From Information to Transformation: Education for the Evolution of Consciousness.* New York: P. Lang, 2001.

———. *The Secret Spiritual World of Children.* Makawao, HI: Inner Ocean Publishing, 2003.

Hawkins, Gary. "Field of Dreams: In the Field." *Kennebec Journal Morning Sentinel,*

3 June 2006, IC.

Helfand, D. J. "What Are the Benefits of Interdisciplinary Education?" *Erudito* (2010). eruditojournal.org/?page_id=163.

Hern, Matt. *Everywhere All the Time: A New Deschooling Reader.* Oakland, CA: AK Press, 2008.

Holt, John. *How Children Fail.* New York: Pitman Publishing Corporation, 1964.

———. *How Children Learn.* New York: Pitman Publishing Corporation, 1967.

———. *The Underachieving School.* New York: Pitman Publishing Corporation, 1969.

———. *What Do I Do Monday?* New York: E. P. Dutton & Company, 1970.

———. *Instead of Education: Ways to Help People Do Things Better.* New York: E. P. Dutton & Company, 1976.

Howe, Neil, and William Strauss. *Millennials Rising: The Next Great Generation.* New York: Vintage Books, 2000.

Jensen, Eric P. "A Fresh Look at Brain-Based Education." *PDK International* 89, 6th ser. (2008): 408–17.

———. *Brain-Based Learning: The New Paradigm of Teaching.* Thousand Oaks, CA: Corwin Press, 2008.

———. *Teaching with the Brain in Mind.* Alexandria, VA: Association for Supervision and Curriculum Development, 1998.

Jones, Casey. *Interdisciplinary Approach—Advantages, Disadvantages, and the Future Benefits of Interdisciplinary Studies* (1 April 2010).

dc.cod.edu/cgi/viewcontent.cgi?article=1121&context=
essai&sei-redir=1&referer=http%3A%2F%2F.

Kaufman, Eric K., J. Shane Robinson, Kimberly A. Bellah,
Cindy Akers, Penny Haase-Wittler, and Lynn
Martindale. "Engaging Students with Brain-Based
Learning" (Research report). *Techniques* 83, no. 6
(January 2008).
www.acteonline.org/uploadedFiles/Publications_and_O
nline_Media/files/files-techniques-2008/Research-
Report-September-2008.pdf,

Keeton, Morris T., and Cooperative Assessment of Experiential
Learning (Project). *Experiential Learning.* San
Francisco: Jossey-Bass Publishers, 1976.

Kelly, F. S., T. McCain, and I. Jukes. *Teaching the Digital
Generation: No More Cookie-Cutter High Schools.*
Thousand Oaks, CA: Corwin Press, 2009.

Kessler, Rachael. *The Soul of Education: Helping Students
Find Connection, Compassion, and Character at
School.* Alexandria, VA: Association for Supervision
and Curriculum Development, 2000.

Kohn, Alfie. *The Homework Myth: Why Our Kids Get Too
Much of a Bad Thing.* Cambridge, MA: Da Capo Life
Long, 2006.

———. *The Schools Our Children Deserve: Moving beyond
Traditional Classrooms and "Tougher Standards."*
Boston, MA: Houghton Mifflin, 1999.

Kolb, A. Y., and David A. Kolb. "Learning Styles and
Learning Spaces: Enhancing Experiential Learning in
Higher Education." *Academy of Management Learning
& Education* 4, no. 2 (2005): 193–212.

Krishnamurti, Jiddu. *Education and the Significance of Life.*
New York: Harper & Row, 1953.

Louv, Richard. *Last Child in the Woods: Saving Our Children
from Nature-Deficit Disorder.* Chapel Hill, NC:
Algonquin Books of Chapel Hill, 2008.

Mack-Kirschner, Adrienne. *Powerful Classroom Stories from Accomplished Teachers*. Thousand Oaks, CA: Corwin Press, 2004.

Mallett, Ronald. *Time Traveler: A Scientist's Personal Mission to Make Time Travel a Reality*. New York: Thunder's Mouth Press, 2006.

Markus, G. B., J. P. F. Howard, and D. C. King. "Integrating Community Service and Classroom Instruction Enhances Learning: Results from an Experiment." *Educational Evaluation and Policy Analysis* 15, no. 4 (January 1993): 410–19.

Martin, Rachel. *Listening Up: Reinventing Ourselves as Teachers and Students*. Portsmouth, NH: Boynton/Cook-Heinemann, 2001.

Miller, Ron. *Free Schools, Free People: Education and Democracy after the 1960s*. Albany, NY: State University of New York Press, 2002.

Morse, Jennifer Roback. "Good Sex: Why We Need More of It and a Lot Less of the Bad Stuff." *American Enterprise*, April 2006.

Neuschwander, T.B., Cutrone, J., Marcias, B.R., Cutrone, S., Murthy, G., Chambers, H., and Hargens, A.R. (2010). The effect of backpacks on the lumbar spine of children: A Standing magnetic resonance imaging study. *Spine Journal*, 35(1), 83-88.

O'Sullivan, E. V., A. Morrell, and M. A. O'Connor. *Expanding the Boundaries of Transformative Learning: Essays on Theory and Praxis*. New York: Palgrave, 2002.

Palmer, Parker J. *The Courage to Teach: Exploring the Inner Landscape of a Teacher's Life*. San Francisco, CA: Jossey-Bass, 1998.

Palmer, Parker J., and Arthur Zajonc. *The Heart of Higher Education: A Call to Renewal*. San Francisco, CA: Jossey-Bass, 2010.

Perkins, David N. *Archimedes' Bathtub: The Art and Logic of Breakthrough Thinking.* New York: W. W. Norton & Co., 2000.

———. *Making Learning Whole: How Seven Principles of Teaching Can Transform Education.* San Francisco, CA: Jossey-Bass, 2009.

Pinker, Steven. "Steven Pinker on Language and Thought" (Video file). July 2005. www.ted.com/talks/steven_pinker_on_language_and_th ought.html.

Posner, M. I., and M. K. Rothbart. *Educating the Human Brain.* Washington, DC: American Psychological Association, 2007.

Proefriedt, William A. *High Expectations: The Cultural Roots of Standards Reform in American Education.* New York: Teachers College Press, 2008.

Pugsley, K. E., and L. H. Clayton. "Traditional Lecture or Experiential Learning: Changing Student Attitudes." *The Journal of Nursing Education* 42, no. 11 (1 January 2003): 520–3.

Rainer, Thomas S., and Jess W. Rainer. *The Millennials: Connecting to America's Largest Generation.* Nashville, TN: B&H Publishing Group, 2011.

Ravitch, Diane. *The Death and Life of the Great American School System: How Testing and Choice Are Undermining Education.* New York: Basic Books, 2010.

Restak, Richard M. *The New Brain: How the Modern Age Is Rewiring Your Mind.* Emmaus, PA: Rodale, 2003.

———. *The Secret Life of the Brain.* Washington, DC: Joseph Henry Press, 2001.

Reynolds, Gretchen. "The Fittest Brains: How Exercising Affects Kids' Intelligence." *New York Times Magazine,* 15 September 2010, 28.

Rhoten, Diane, Veronica Boix Mansilla, Marc Chun, and Julie Thompson Klein. "Interdisciplinary Education at

Liberal Arts Institutions." *Teagle Foundation White Paper*. New York: Teagle Foundation, n.d. www.evergreen.edu/washcenter/resources/upload/2006s srcwhitepaper.pdf.

Robinson, Ken. *Out of Our Minds: Learning to Be Creative*. Oxford, UK: Capstone Publishing Limited, 2001.

——— "Sir Ken Robinson: Do Schools Kill Creativity?" TED Talk, 6 January 2007. youtube/iG9CE55wbtY

———. "Sir Ken Robinson: Bring on the Learning Revolution!" TED Talk, May 2010. www.ted.com/talks/sir_ken_robinson_bring_on_the_re volution.html

Robinson, Ken, and Lou Aronica. *The Element: How Finding Your Passion Changes Everything*. New York: Viking, 2009.

Rosen, Larry D., Mark L. Carrier, and Nancy A. Cheever. *Rewired: Understanding the iGeneration and the Way They Learn*. New York: Palgrave Macmillan, 2010.

RSA Organization. "RSA Animate: Changing Education Paradigms" (Video file). 14 October 2010. youtube/zDZFcDGpL4U.

Sapolsky, Robert. "This Is Your Brain on Metaphors." *New York Times*, Opinionator, 14 November 2010. opinionator.blogs.nytimes.com/2010/11/14/this-is-your-brain-on-metaphors/?hp.

Seventh Generation Education. *The Library of Halexandriah*. Halexandria Foundation, n.d. Retrieved from halexandria.org/dward038.htm.

Shallcross, D. "Thanks Sen. Rosenberg for Creativity Legislation." *Daily Hampshire Gazette*, 25 August 2010, A6.

Sethi, Kiran Bir. "Kiran Bir Sethi Teaches Kids to Take Charge" (Video file). www.ted.com/talks/kiran_bir_sethi_teaches_kids_to_ta ke_charge.html.

Sipos, Yona, Bryce Battisti, and Kurt Grimm. "Achieving Transformative Sustainability Learning: Engaging Head, Hands, and Heart." *International Journal of Sustainability in Higher Education* 9, no. 1 (11 April 2007): 68–86. DOI: 10.1108/14676370810842193.

Smilkstein, Rita. *We're Born to Learn: Using the Brain's Natural Learning Process to Create Today's Curriculum.* Thousand Oaks, CA: Corwin Press, 2003.

Sousa, David A. *How the Brain Learns: A Classroom Teacher's Guide*, 2nd ed. Thousand Oaks, CA: Corwin Press, 2001.

———. *How the Brain Learns*, 3rd ed. Thousand Oaks, CA: Corwin Press, 2006.

Sternberg, Robert J. "Interdisciplinary Problem-Based Learning: An Alternative to Traditional Majors and Minors." *Liberal Education* 94, no. 1 (2008): 12–17.

Strauss, William, and Neil Howe. *Generations: The History of America's Future, 1584 to 2069.* New York: William Morrow and Co., 1991.

Suárez-Orozco, Marcelo M. *Learning in the Global Era: International Perspectives on Globalization and Education.* Berkeley, CA: University of California Press, 2007.

Sylwester, Robert. *A Celebration of Neurons: An Educator's Guide to the Human Brain.* Alexandria, VA: Association for Supervision and Curriculum Development, 1995.

Thomas, Michael. *Deconstructing Digital Natives: Young People, Technology, and the New Literacies.* New York: Routledge, 2011.

Wagner, Tony. *The Global Achievement Gap: Why Even Our Best Schools Don't Teach the New Survival Skills Our Children Need—and What We Can Do About It.* New York: Basic Books, 2008.

"Washington Teen Fakes Pregnancy as School Project."
Weekend Daily Hampshire Gazette, 23–24 April 2011,
A8.

Whitby, Greg. "Twenty-First-Century Pedagogy" (Video).
29 September 2007,
www.youtube.com/watch?v=l72UFXqa8ZU.

Willis, Judy. "Building a Bridge from Neuroscience to the
Classroom." *Phi Delta Kappan* 89, no. 6 (1 February
2008): 424–7.

Winograd, Morley, and Michael D. Hais. *Millennial
Momentum: How a New Generation Is Remaking
America*. New Brunswick, NJ: Rutgers University
Press, 2011.

Zull, James E. *The Art of Changing the Brain: Enriching
Teaching by Exploring the Biology of Learning*.
Sterling, VA: Stylus Publishing, 2002.

Acknowledgments

First and foremost I wish to thank, with love, my students who taught me so much about a myriad of interesting topics. It is you who inspired me to write this book that will, I hope, inspire those who read it.

I am grateful to Sophia Lai who kept me researching and writing. Special thanks goes to Nikki Tishler for her interdisciplinary perspective and her love of the book. I thank heaven for Courtney Pitzner, an angel from Ithaca who appeared right when I needed her most. I am indebted to Kate Feldmann, who helped "massage" the manuscript. Heartfelt thanks to my copyeditor Mike Fleming, who got me over the finish line and got the manuscript "in the can."

Special thanks goes Dennis Monroe and Greg Henderson—your support fueled and sustained me. Indelible thanks goes to Steve MacDougall, my mentor and friend in education. My gratitude goes to Don Siviski for advancing the education that is relevant to our times and for urging me to write the stories of the Capstones by asking, "If not you, then who? If not now, then when?"

Special thanks also goes to Paige Doore, a super neighbor and early supporter of the book; to Zina Barden, the first to endorse the idea for the book; and to Alexa Lightner for seeing the best in me. Acknowledgment also goes to those students who steeled my determination for the Capstone to succeed.

Much love and thanks to my son, Toby Aronson, who inspires me with his capacity to create, and to my daughter, Angela Aronson, who inspires me with her capacity to love. I am most grateful to my husband, Richard A. Aronson, my most trusted listener and greatest supporter.

About the Author

Linda Aronson, OTR, M.Ed. is an innovator and leader in the field of education, first as a school-based occupational therapist and more recently as the creator and facilitator of a high school Senior Seminar and Senior Capstone initiative. She is a registered occupational therapist and certified in English Language Arts at the secondary level. Linda is a graduate of Tufts University and earned her self-designed, interdisciplinary Master's in Education degree from the University of Vermont. She has lectured widely, led workshops and training in: sensory integration, parenting for spiritual development, the principles and process of creating, brain development and brain-based learning at the community, college, and professional conference levels. Linda has been featured on TV, radio, and in print media. She is the author of the popular and highly acclaimed parenting book *Big Spirits, Little Bodies: Parenting Your Way to Wholeness*, published by A.R.E. Press. A lover of nature, she is a sunrise and sunset catcher. Linda has lived and worked in Ithaca, New York; Boston; Burlington, Vermont; Madison, Wisconsin; Hallowell, Maine; and currently Amherst, Massachusetts.

Workshops available on the Capstone Model, the science of learning, experiential and applied learning, and the principles and process of creating for educators.

Visit website: www.Linda-Aronson.com, e-mail
LindaAronson8@gmail.com, call 207-620-4224.